Why Turkey is

Join the Left Book Club

Membership of the Left Book Club will give you at least four specially selected books each year, plus invitations to author events and discussion groups.

To join, please visit www.leftbookclub.com

Also available

*A People's History of
the Russian Revolution*
Neil Faulkner

*A Party with Socialists in It
A History of the Labour Left*
Simon Hannah
Foreword by John McDonnell

*Being Red
A Politics for the Future*
Ken Livingstone

*Syriza
Inside the Labyrinth*
Kevin Ovenden
Foreword by Paul Mason

*Student Revolt
Voices of the Austerity Generation*
Matt Myers
Foreword by Paul Mason

*Sound System
The Political Power of Music*
Dave Randall

*Cut Out
Living Without Welfare*
Jeremy Seabrook

*The Rent Trap
How We Fell Into It and
How We Get Out of It*
Rosie Walker and Samir Jeraj

Why Turkey is Authoritarian

From Atatürk to Erdoğan

Halil Karaveli

PLUTO PRESS

First published 2018 by Pluto Press
345 Archway Road, London N6 5AA

www.plutobooks.com

Copyright © Halil Karaveli 2018

The right of Halil Karaveli to be identified as the author of this work has
been asserted by him in accordance with the Copyright, Designs and
Patents Act 1988.

The Left Book Club pays homage to the original Left Book Club founded by
Victor Gollancz in 1936.

British Library Cataloguing in Publication Data
A catalogue record for this book is available from the British Library

ISBN	978 0 7453 3756 2	Hardback
ISBN	978 0 7453 3755 5	Paperback
ISBN	978 1 7868 0265 1	PDF eBook
ISBN	978 1 7868 0267 5	Kindle eBook
ISBN	978 1 7868 0266 8	EPUB eBook

This book is printed on paper suitable for recycling and made from fully
managed and sustained forest sources. Logging, pulping and manufacturing
processes are expected to conform to the environmental standards of the
country of origin.

Typeset by Stanford DTP Services, Northampton, England

Simultaneously printed in the United Kingdom and United States of America

This book is dedicated to Saga Karaveli

Contents

Series Preface   ix
Timeline   xi
List of Illustrations   xv

Introduction   1
1   A Pattern of Violence   9
2   Kemalism and the Left   35
3   Capitalist Foundation   70
4   How the Right Won the People   105
5   Social Democratic Hope   129
6   Vengeance of the Right   162
7   The Rise of the Islamists   188
Epilogue: Class, Identity and Democracy   209
Afterword: Attacking the Kurds – The 'Return'
    of Kemalism   213

Notes   220
Bibliography   226
Index   228

CONTENTS

Series Preface

The first Left Book Club (1936–48) had 57,000 members, had distributed two million books, and had formed 1,200 workplace and local groups by the time it peaked in 1939. LBC members were active throughout the labour and radical movement at the time, and the Club became an educational mass movement, remodelling British public opinion and contributing substantially to the Labour landslide of 1945 and the construction of the welfare state.

Publisher Victor Gollancz, the driving force, saw the LBC as a movement against poverty, fascism, and the growing threat of war. He aimed to resist the tide of austerity and appeasement, and to present radical ideas for progressive social change in the interests of working people. The Club was about enlightenment, empowerment, and collective organisation.

The world today faces a crisis on the scale of the 1930s. Capitalism is trapped in a long-term crisis. Financialisation and austerity are shrinking demand, deepening the depression, and widening social inequalities. The social fabric is being torn apart. International relations are increasingly tense and militarised. War threatens on several fronts, while fascist and racist organisations are gaining ground across much of Europe. Global warming threatens the planet and the whole of humanity with climate catastrophe. Workplace organisation has been weakened, and social democratic parties have been hollowed out by acceptance of pro-market dogma. Society has become more atomised, and mainstream politics suffers an acute democratic deficit.

Yet the last decade has seen historically unprecedented levels of participation in street protest, implying a mass audience for progressive alternatives. But socialist ideas are no longer, as in the immediate post-war period, 'in the tea'. One of neoliberalism's achievements has been to undermine ideas of solidarity, collective provision, and public service.

The Left Book Club aspires to meet this ideological challenge. Our aim is to offer high-quality books at affordable prices that are carefully selected to address the central issues of the day and to be accessible to a wide general audience. Our list represents the full range of progressive traditions, perspectives, and ideas. We hope the books will be used as the basis of reading circles, discussion groups, and other educational and cultural activities relevant to developing, sharing, and disseminating ideas for change in the interests of the common people at home and abroad.

Timeline

1000 (ca.) Turkic tribes from Central Asia begin to enter Anatolia, the peninsula of which the present state of Turkey mostly consists.

1299 (ca.) The Turkic chieftain Osman founds the emirate that will later expand into the Ottoman Empire.

1838 The Ottoman government signs a free-trade agreement with Great Britain, soon followed by similar treaties with several other European states, that turns the Ottoman lands into an open market for European products, ruining local crafts and industry.

1839 Under the pressure of European powers, the Ottoman government declares the legal equality of all subjects, regardless of their religion.

1876 The Ottoman state becomes a constitutional monarchy.

1878 Sultan Abdülhamid II suspends the constitution and reinstitutes despotic rule.

1881 The former grand vizier (prime minister) Mithat Pasha, the author of the liberal constitution of 1876 and the first social and democratic reformer in Ottoman history, is put to death in his prison cell, likely on the orders of the Sultan Abdülhamid II.

1908 The Young Turk revolution. The constitutional order is restored and the parliament is reopened.

1914 The Ottoman Empire, ruled by the nationalist Young Turks, enters the First World War on the side of Germany and Austria-Hungary.

1915 The Armenian genocide. Around 1 million Ottoman Armenians are estimated to have been put to death by the Young Turk regime.

1919–1923 The Anatolian war: Turkish national forces led by Mustafa Kemal, later Atatürk, fight occupying Greek and French forces, but also the indigenous Greeks and Armenians of Anatolia.

1921 The leadership of Communist Party of Turkey is massacred, in all likelihood on the orders of the nationalist leader Mustafa Kemal.

1922 The Ottoman sultanate is abolished.

1923 The Republic of Turkey is founded. The entire Greek Orthodox population of Anatolia, over 1 million, is expelled from the new state of Turkey after an agreement between Turkey and Greece. Greece expels several hundred thousand Muslims to Turkey.

1937–1938 Tens of thousands of Kurds in the province of Dersim are massacred by the Turkish army and air force.

1950 The first free election is held. The conservative Democrat Party comes to power.

1960 Turkey's first military coup takes place.

1961 Parliamentary rule is restored.

1963 Workers are accorded collective bargaining rights and the right to strike.

1971 A right-wing military coup is staged to pre-empt a planned left-wing military coup.

1975 The start of a fascist campaign of mass violence. Thousands of left-wing students, teachers, intellectuals and activists are killed between 1975 and 1980. The fascist militia acts with impunity, protected by right-wing governments and the military. The first attempt to kill Bülent Ecevit, the social democratic leader, is made.

1977 Workers celebrating 1 May are massacred in Taksim square in Istanbul. Social democrats win the parliamentary election.

1978 In a pogrom in the city of Kahramanmaraş, the fascist militia, abetted by the police and the military, massacres several hundred Alevis, a left-leaning religious minority.

1980–1983 Right-wing military dictatorship. Hundreds of thousands of leftists are imprisoned. Several hundred are tortured to death. The junta imposes a neoliberal economic regime and bolsters Islamic influence as a counterweight to the left.

1997 The first Islamist-led government of Turkey is forced to resign after pressure from the military and the state establishment.

2001 Islamists who want to have good relations with the United States and the European Union, and who are supported by the business circles in Turkey, form the conservative Justice and Development Party (AKP).

2002 The AKP comes to power.

2007 The Armenian-Turkish journalist Hrant Dink is assassinated.

2015 Over 100 Turkish and Kurdish leftist peace activists are killed in a terrorist attack in Ankara.

2016 A faction of the military tries to overthrow President Recep Tayyip Erdoğan, but the coup attempt, which is tacitly supported by the United States, fails.

2016 Selahattin Demirtaş, the co-leader of the pro-Kurdish and socialist Peoples' Democratic Party, is imprisoned along with other leading cadres of the party.

List of Illustrations

Figure 1. The newly elected president Mustafa Kemal, among religious and other notables on a tour in Anatolia in 1924   39

Figure 2. The conservative prime minister Adnan Menderes in rural Anatolia   106

Figure 3. Hat off for the people: the conservative leader Süleyman Demirel   108

Figure 4. Social democratic hope: the centre-left leader Bülent Ecevit   130

Figure 5. Ecevit in his characteristic Jeff cap, worn by the peasants in Anatolia   141

Figure 6. Mimicking Hitler: Alparslan Türkeş, the Turkish fascist leader   167

Figure 7. Necmettin Erbakan, the father of political Islam in Turkey   192

Figure 8. One with the people: Recep Tayyip Erdoğan has claimed to represent the interests of the popular classes   198

All images are reproduced courtesy of the archive of the Directorate General of Press and Information, Republic of Turkey Office of the Prime Minister.

Introduction

Turkey is the kind of country that exercises a distinct fascination. But it is also a country that lends itself all too easily to exoticism. Turkey is invariably a place where 'East meets West', where secularism and 'Westernization' fatefully collide with Islam. For the last century, the Western world has regarded Turkey as a pivotal case of the 'clash of civilizations' between Islam and the West. But East and West are slippery categories, and there is another story to be told, one obscured by the 'clash of civilizations' and the tug of war between secularism and Islam, and which explains why Turkey is authoritarian: the continuity of right-wing rule. This book will shift attention away from 'clashes' and ruptures to the structures – social, economic and ideological – that have sustained an undemocratic regime, from the secularist Mustafa Kemal Atatürk, the founder of the Turkish republic, to the Islamist Recep Tayyip Erdoğan, who, superficially, represents his antithesis.

Turkey was a nationalist-bourgeois one-party dictatorship from its founding in 1923 until 1950, when the first free election was held. And it has remained a bourgeois regime. Some readers will object to this terminology – why bourgeois? – but it is crucial to recognize the class character of the Turkish regime. It is occulted in the standard histories, but as this book will show, the interests of the class that owns the means of production have been decisive in shaping Turkey's historical journey, to the detriment of the development of democracy. The founders of the state, the military officers and bureaucrats, specifically endeavoured to create what they called a 'national bourgeoisie'; indeed, as will become clear in what follows, this was their overriding objective. From 1960 to 1961 and from 1971 to 1973 the military was in direct charge, but its rule during these periods was tempered; not every political party was banned, and in the later period the elected parliament remained open as well. From 1980 to 1983, Turkey was a full-blown, right-wing military dictatorship. Let us be precise: it was a neoliberal and nationalist dictatorship. Otherwise, the rulers of the country have enjoyed democratic legitimacy. Yet a fully developed democracy has nonetheless continued to elude Turkey, and democratically elected leaders have trampled on freedoms and resorted to oppression. Erdoğan is the latest example of such a ruler. His regime has been described as an example of 'illiberal democracy'. But, clearly, Turkey's political regime has overall been characterized by one form or another of authoritarianism, running from the most unrestrained, with no tolerance for any free expression of the people's will, to more 'tempered' versions with a semblance of democracy; hence the title of this book.

I will argue that the answer to the question why Turkey has remained authoritarian is to be found in the permanence of right-wing rule and in the dynamics of capitalism that have destabilized democracy. The right has come in different incarnations – secularist or Islamic – but always with the same mission, to protect the dominant economic interests from democratic challenges, from the broad masses of the people. A closer look reveals that secularists and Islamists are in fact two sides of the right. And for most of the time, there has been no proper left with a mass following to challenge authoritarian right-wing power.

Anyone who has followed international politics even casually during the last couple of decades will be familiar with what is in fact a fictitious narrative: media and 'experts' have been telling us that, in Turkey, the military stages coups, or used to stage them, in order to 'protect secularism'. Yet the truth is that the Turkish military and the Islamists have more in common than appearances would suggest. Overall, they have both served capital. Neither has the main axis of conflict in Turkish politics been that between the military and civilians, as the standard history holds. Whether ruled by secularists or Islamists, by the military or by the civilian right, Turkey has fundamentally remained the same: nationalism and capitalism have been the pillars of what has always been a right-wing regime, albeit with varying accents of cultural and religious conservatism.

When in 2007 Turkey was for the first time about to elect a president whose wife wore the Islamic headscarf, hundreds of thousands of secularist Turks took to the streets in mass protests. They marched carrying huge portraits of Atatürk. They idolize him because they believe that Atatürk, in the words of his British biographer Patrick Kinross, 'transported his country from the Middle Ages to the threshold of the modern era and a stage beyond'.[1] They were convinced that the Islamist strongman Erdoğan was going to return Turkey to the Middle Ages. Yet while ordinary, secular middle- and upper-class Turks were traumatized by the prospect of having a first lady who wears the Islamic headscarf, it was 'business as usual' for the secular big barons of Turkish capitalism, even though they are also 'Westernized' in the sense that the word is understood in Turkey: they use alcohol, and their spouses do not cover their heads. Yet the 'Westernized' circles of

Turkish big business endorsed Erdoğan early on. His religious conservatism was never an issue for them; on the contrary, it was, as one business patron pointed out, an asset. Many in the West believed that Erdoğan was going to bring democracy to Turkey; they have been thoroughly disappointed. But Erdoğan has lived up to his pledge to capitalism, pursuing the business-friendly policies he had promised he would execute.

Turkey has from the beginning been an inhospitable terrain for the left. Oppression has always been severe. But that is not the whole story; oppression is not the only reason why the left has been crippled. In a 2016 survey, two thirds of the population of Turkey identified themselves as pious, nationalist and conservative and less than one third as either leftists, social democrats or socialists. As a rule, the masses have rallied to populist conservatives who on the campaign trail have spoken to their religious feelings and resentment of the elite, while in power serving the interests of that elite. So, what's the matter with Turkey? In fact, the country is not unique.

In his now classic account, *What's the Matter With Kansas? How Conservatives Won the Heart of America* (2004), the American journalist Thomas Frank described the French Revolution in reverse that has taken place in the United States since the 1990s, where the *sans culottes* have poured down the streets demanding more power to the aristocracy, electing plutocrats to the White House. Frank described how the right has marshalled popular cultural anger to secure the economic privileges of the rich, how the poor vote against their own economic self-interest because they are distracted by social and cultural issues like gay marriage, abortion and guns – questions that have alienated the working class from the progressives. The left in Turkey has similarly been crippled because, historically, it has been identified with opposition to religion and tradition, which has isolated it from the broad masses, the workers and the peasants.

The Turkish left has come with a heavy baggage: the secularist legacy of the founding, Kemalist era of the country. Socialists and social democrats, and occasionally even Marxists, pledge allegiance to Kemalism. It was a revolution from above, carried out by middle-class, state cadres, that made Turkey, and this has shaped progressive thinking. Social and labour issues, the concerns of the working class, have taken a backseat to middle-class radical priorities: progress, 'enlightenment', modernization and nation-building. The Kemalist left has not only been incapable of challenging the dominance of the right because it has been disconnected from the popular classes; its embrace of nationalism and statism has also legitimized and served to sustain an authoritarian political culture. Its nationalism has if anything exacerbated the ethnic polarization of Turks and Kurds. As we will see, leftists of this particular mould have tragically even made common cause with the nationalist far right.

The historical record of comparable countries like Greece, Spain and Portugal illustrates that social democracy plays a crucial role in the passage from right-wing authoritarianism to democracy. In the 1970s, when these other southern European nations were moving toward democracy, social democracy was on the rise in Turkey as well. It was, as we shall see, a European-style social democracy that reinvented the progressive tradition of Turkey; it challenged inequality and social injustice, rather than religious culture and tradition, and it was therefore successful. But Turkey was not allowed to follow the paths of Greece, Spain and Portugal. Between 1975 and 1980, the left was crushed by the onslaught of the right: fascist death-squads and a brutal military dictatorship extinguished hopes for freedom and social justice. The vengeance of the right ensured that the interests of the capitalist class – and, not unimportantly, the strategic interests of the United States – were safeguarded. The Turkish left of the time was a casualty of the dynamics of capitalism and of the Cold War; Islamic conservatism has been their beneficiary.

The left has never recovered from that devastating blow. Turkey's main opposition party today calls itself social democratic and is a member of the Socialist International; yet it is still to find a way to win over the working class from the right. The Republican People's Party (CHP) was founded by Atatürk himself, and is secularist-nationalist rather than social democrat; it has its main support base among the secular middle class and it shows scant interest for working-class issues. 'We are the soldiers of Mustafa Kemal' is a favourite slogan among party activists today.

The other main strain of the Turkish left is a liberal left that ignores the working-class perspective as well. While the Kemalist left has embraced the state as an engine of progress, its antithesis, the liberal left, is an advocate of 'bourgeois revolution', maintaining that the middle class will bring democracy to Turkey. When Erdoğan's party, which is supported by both the middle class and the working class, rose to power, the liberal left rejoiced; in the words of one leading, self-professed socialist intellectual, 'a real bourgeois revolution' had finally taken place in Turkey.[2] Incongruously, the liberal leftist intellectuals championed the Islamic right because it represented a class that they assumed had a vested interest in political liberalization: a new, 'globalized' bourgeoisie, a rising class of businessmen and industrialists. The tragedy of the two dominant strains of what passes for the left in Turkey is that they have both legitimized right-wing authoritarianism; the Kemalist left by embracing nationalism and statism, and the so-called liberal left by cheering on an Islamic right that was held to be liberal.

Turkey is yet another case illustrating that freedom for capital certainly does not translate into political freedom, as liberal theory has held for the last two centuries. On the contrary, as we will see in what follows, dominant economic interests have historically interplayed with and helped to sustain authoritarian rule in Turkey, regardless of whether the regime has been secular or Islamic. Ultimately, Turkish history is instructive for a left facing the global challenge of a rising populist right, which succeeds in mobilizing culture and identity for its own purposes. The story of Turkey – where the right has, for most of the time, succeeded in monopolizing the working-class vote by playing on religion and culture – is being replicated across Europe and in the United States. The European and American centre-left's inability to hold on to their working-class base paves the way for the far right. In many countries, social democrats have abandoned the working class, as traditional social democracy has merged with neoliberalism and globalized free-market policies since the 1980s. But serving the interests of global capitalism is not paying off electorally: in 2016, European social democratic parties lost 12 out of 18 national elections. In the 2017 elections in Germany, which saw the far right surge, the social democrats collapsed, turning in their worst performance since the Second World War with little more than 20 per cent of the vote. There is a growing awareness that the solution lies in returning to the core strengths of the left, that the best thing the left can do is fight its own battles for social rights, solidarity and equality. Yet in an age of cultural anxieties, fed by austerity and terror alerts, far-right populism offers an intoxicating brew; the far right has become the party of the working class in countries like France and Sweden.

Turkey is a warning example: it shows how the left can be disabled when the right succeeds in recasting class conflict as culture war, exploiting the detachment between the popular classes, the uneducated rural population and the working class, and the urban elites. The future of democracy will depend on the emergence of a reinvigorated left that embraces the cause of the people, of the working class and of minorities, and which by speaking up for social justice and freedom succeeds in reconciling social and cultural claims. It is particularly useful to ponder the Turkish case, because it illustrates the fact that the left must be able to connect culturally with the popular masses if it is to make a difference.

CHAPTER ONE

A Pattern of Violence

'This is a Bloodstained Square'

The moment the first of the two bombs goes off is captured on a video clip: a group of young people are joined together in an embrace, performing a traditional Anatolian folk dance. Eerily, they are singing 'This is a bloodstained square'. They exude happiness, however, and the atmosphere is festive. Then, suddenly, there is a blast behind them. There are flames, and the blue, sunny sky is shrouded by a cloud of smoke that quickly expands. The dancers cast a quick glance backwards before diving for cover. The picture is blurred.

On 10 October 2015, over one hundred leftist peace activists, Turks and Kurds, were blown up in Ankara. They were assembling on the square next to the train station in Ankara when the two suicide bombers struck. The activists had heeded the calls of several trade unions and of the pro-Kurdish and socialist Peoples' Democratic Party (HDP) to protest against the war that the Turkish military was waging against Turkey's own Kurdish citizens in the south-east of the country, laying waste to entire towns. The massacre in Ankara is the deadliest terrorist attack in Turkey to date. Yet it was anything but atypical in terms of what it stood for politically. The carnage fitted all too well into a pattern of mass killings since the late 1960s: the victims are invariably leftists, other democrats, or ethnic and religious minorities. The perpetrators are drawn from the country's deep, popular reservoir of ultra-conservatives and ultra-nationalists. Those who commission the massacres and the assassinations lurk in the shadows.

The Ankara massacre followed on the killing of over 30 young socialists in a suicide bombing a few months earlier. On both occasions, the authorities identified the perpetrators as Turkish citizens who they claimed had acted on behalf of the so-called 'Islamic State'. The latter, however, did not claim responsibility for the Ankara massacre. Progressives and liberals felt they had good reason to suspect that the suicide bombers in Ankara had acted with the encouragement, or at very least the protection, of the Turkish state. To many, it seemed obvious that history was repeating itself, that elements of the infamous Turkish 'deep state' – the right-wing networks of conspirators and assassins embedded within the state – had been reactivated to crush the Kurdish and Turkish left. Hasan Cemal, a prominent liberal journalist, wrote that he harboured no doubt at all that President Erdoğan's regime had brought the instruments of the deep state back into use.

The lyrics of the song that was interrupted at the peace rally in Ankara in 2015 – 'This is a bloodstained square' – referred to Beyazıt Square in Istanbul, where two young leftist demonstrators were slain by a fascist mob on 16 February 1969. Establishing a pattern that was to be repeated many times, the police stood by passively, and the perpetrators, none of whom were brought to justice, were defended by a right-wing government that blamed the victims for what had happened. In the same vein, the Islamic conservative government in 2015 displayed no empathy for the victims, instead accusing the organizers of the rally of having deliberately willed the carnage, supposedly with the purpose of destabilizing the government. Again in accordance with the historical pattern, no security measures whatsoever had been taken to protect the rally, and, according to the Association of Turkish Doctors, the intervention of the police – firing tear gas over the site of the massacre – caused the deaths of several of the wounded.

The 'Bloodstained Sunday' of 1969, as it became known, was immortalized by the left-wing folk singer Ruhi Su. The cultural life of Turkey has historically been dominated by the left, but the Turkish state has also been pitiless in its persecution of those who have been the leading embodiments of the country's culture, and Su was no exception. He was pursuing a career at the Turkish State Opera when in 1952 he was sentenced to prison for five years for having been a member of the banned Communist Party of Turkey (TKP). The Turkish state persecuted Su until his death, indeed caused it. Diagnosed with cancer, he applied for a passport in order to be able to travel to Europe for treatment; his request was turned down, and when the authorities finally acquiesced, it was too late for him to be cured. The 'Bloodstained Sunday' that Ruhi Su helped to immortalize was the starting point of a decade of right-wing violence. Its purpose was to intimidate the left and derail the social democratic movement that was on the rise during the first half of the 1970s. These goals were achieved. The violence in Turkey during the 1970s drew little international attention, and this is also a period that is glossed over in accounts of modern Turkish history. Yet it was a momentous era, and we will return to it later.

On International Labour Day in 1977, Istanbul's Taksim Square was the site of carnage. A crowd of several hundred thousand had gathered when unidentified assassins opened fire from the high-rise blocks that surround the square. At least 40 were killed. In 1978, hundreds of Alevis were massacred in the cities of Kahramanmaraş and Çorum. The Alevis are heterodox Muslims whose syncretistic creed amalgamates elements of Shiite Islam, pre-Islamic traditions and Anatolian popular culture; in social terms, they have historically belonged to the underprivileged. They are estimated to make up perhaps as much as 15 to 20 per cent of the population of Turkey, and there are Turkish as well as Kurdish Alevis. The Alevis have been the victims of social and religious discrimination and oppression for centuries, from the days of Ottoman rule up to the present. This has made them a natural, left-leaning constituency; they present a parallel to the similarly socially underprivileged and traditionally oppressed Shiites in Iraq and Lebanon, who used to provide communist parties with a strong popular base in those countries. Hasan Fehmi Güneş, a social democrat who served as interior minister in 1978, later bore witness that the National Intelligence Agency of the state had in fact armed and directed the Sunni mob that carried out the massacres of the Alevis. The complicity, or at the very least criminal negligence, of the Turkish state was again on display in 1993: this time, Alevis and leftists were attacked by a Sunni mob in the city of Sivas. A hotel where a group of leftist writers – most of whom were Alevis – had gathered for a culture event, was set on fire. The police and the gendarmerie passively stood by, doing nothing to disperse the mob or to prevent it from starting the fire. Thirty-five were killed.

As just noted, the campaign of fascist violence in the 1970s went largely unnoticed by international opinion; the contrast is stark between lack of attention given to the 1977 Labour

Day massacre on Istanbul's Taksim Square and the international reaction in 2013 to the crushing of the Gezi protests, the environmentalist action to save the park that borders the square. The Gezi protests and their crushing became a world event. The action initiated by a middle-class, radical youth swelled into a popular mass protest when the working class, mostly Alevis, joined the rallies in Istanbul and across Turkey. Not coincidentally, all of the casualties – 14 protesters were killed by the police – were Alevis. Hundreds of the protesters suffered serious injuries, many of them losing eyes. The Gezi protests were a turning point: the ruthless violence deployed against peaceful protesters ruined the international image of Erdoğan, a conservative who until then had been taken to be a democratic reformer by global, liberal opinion. Only a year earlier the US president Barack Obama had listed Erdoğan among the five world leaders with whom he said he had been able to forge 'friendships and the bonds of trust'. The Gezi events spoiled the Obama-Erdoğan relationship. The US president was reported to be deeply disappointed; more importantly, Erdoğan had now become a political liability, and for a time Obama refused to take any phone calls from his once trusted friend.

For years, the general consensus among international observers was that Erdoğan's mission was to make Turkey democratic. This belief reflected a deep ignorance of Turkish history. Otherwise it would not have come as a surprise that yet another Turkish conservative leader turned out to be an authoritarian who did not flinch from using violence against leftists and minorities. But the fundamental, right-wing character of the repression and state violence in Turkey is rarely, if ever, recognized in the standard histories. The fact that

Turkey is authoritarian is conventionally accounted for either by the putative secularist ambitions of the erstwhile so-called Kemalist state elite or, as is recently the case with Erdoğan's regime, by the Islamist ideology of its rulers. The right-wing continuity from Kemalists to Islamists is never acknowledged.

'May those who love the fatherland strike at the communists!' Thus exhorted the mouthpiece of the one-party regime of the Republican People's Party, *Vatan*, on 3 December 1945. Readers of the *Vatan* editorial well understood who the 'communists' in question were: the publishers of the left-wing daily *Tan*. The newspaper had drawn the ire of the regime of President İsmet İnönü, who had succeeded Kemal Atatürk in 1938, because it called for better relations between Turkey and the Soviet Union. In the eyes of the regime, it was a fifth column. This was a time when Joseph Stalin, emboldened after the Soviet victory in the Second World War, postured aggressively against Turkey, to which the İnönü regime was responding by mounting a witch-hunt against left-wing intellectuals, purging left-wing academics, and by mobilizing religion as a counter-weight to the perceived threat from the left, as I will describe later. The *Vatan* editorial calling for patriots to strike at the communists was distributed among the students at Istanbul University, to immediate effect. The next day, 4 December 1945, the students performed their 'patriotic duty': they marched to and stormed the press of the *Tan* and wrecked it as the police looked on. They continued their rampage by smashing the press of another left-wing publication, owned by the writer Sabahattin Ali, who was murdered by the Turkish secret service three years later. Among the right-wing rioters who heeded the call of the organ of the Kemalist regime were no less than three future presidents and prime ministers,

Süleyman Demirel, Turgut Özal and Necmettin Erbakan, two conservatives and one Islamist. The right-wing parentage of Kemalism, conservatism and Islamism is perfectly illustrated.

At a superficial glance, it would appear that modern Turkish history has been defined by discontinuity, as I noted in the introduction. The country has been ruled by generals and civilians, by secularists and Islamic conservatives; there was a break with Islamic tradition when the state was founded, while lately Islam is held to have triumphed over secularism with Erdoğan. On the face of it, he is the antithesis of the 'founding father' of the Turkish state, Atatürk. But this narrative line misses the political lineage that connects the two. Atatürk was of course a cultural radical, while Erdoğan is a social and cultural conservative, not to say a reactionary. What escapes attention, though, is the affinity of their class politics: Atatürk was a bourgeois radical, while Erdoğan is a bourgeois conservative. These distinctions are obviously not insignificant, but they do not change the fact these are two variants of a bourgeois ideology that has held sway and served the same class interests since the founding of Turkey. The dominant class interests have only been challenged once: Bülent Ecevit, the only social democrat who has served as prime minister of Turkey, mounted a leftist challenge to the system, and typically, he is ignored by the standard history. In this book though, he will be getting the attention that he deserves.

The personalities of political leaders, the contingent nature of politics, and the power struggles within the elite must all be taken into account in exploring the logic of the authoritarianism that has persisted in Turkey. But, as the following pages will make clear, it is capitalist dynamics that, on a structural level, have sustained authoritarianism from Atatürk to Erdoğan.

There is also another historical pattern that stands out: Turkey has a way of generating what turn out to be false hopes. Just as liberals, in Turkey and beyond, expected democratic wonders from Erdoğan, so did leftists entertain illusions about the 'progressive' Atatürk. The country's genesis – its rise out of the ashes of the Ottoman Empire after the First World War – was greeted with high expectations by those, socialists and communists alike, who, as it would turn out, were soon to suffer terribly under a state that was conceived as an engine of bourgeois interests.

In the next section, after a brief historical detour, we will meet the first group of those victims: Mustafa Suphi, the founding leader of the Communist Party of Turkey, and his 14 comrades, who were murdered on 28 January 1921. In hindsight, these brutal murders stand out as an emblematic act of political violence. They were an early revelation of the ideological identity of the state founded by Atatürk, and, in a sense, they set the tone for the violence and repression that has since ensued.

Opening Act: 28 January 1921

Was the Russian Revolution going to be followed by a Turkish Revolution? Along with the Russian Empire and the Romanovs' centuries-old dynasty, and Austria-Hungary, the empire of the Habsburgs, the First World War had also undone the Ottoman Empire, known as the 'sick man of Europe' since the mid nineteenth century. In 1914, the empire included what are now Turkey, Syria, Iraq, Lebanon, Palestine, Jordan, Israel, Saudi Arabia and Yemen. When the war ended in 1918, the same Western powers that rushed to strangle the Bolsheviks in Russia hurried to carve up the territory of the defeated Ottoman Empire and wipe it off the map. David Lloyd George, the British prime minister, no friend of the Turks, was in the driving seat of the endeavour. He encouraged Greece to invade Anatolia. The British and the French divided the Arab provinces between them. They occupied the capital Constantinople. Greek troops took possession of Smyrna (today Izmir), the second largest city, which had a Greek majority.

Thirty-five sultans had succeeded to the throne since their forefather Osman, a tribal chief of Central Asian origin, had founded an emirate at the north-western edge of Anatolia at the end of the thirteenth century. Anatolia, *Anadolu* in Turkish, is the peninsula of which more than 90 per cent of the territory of Turkey consists, except for a small piece of geographically European territory, eastern Thrace. The word Anatolia originates in Greek, and means 'where the sun rises', but for Greeks and Europeans the peninsular region has more commonly been known as Asia Minor. For two millennia, from Antiquity to the twelfth century, when tribes from Central Asia entered the scene, Anatolia was part of the Hellenistic world. It should be noted that present-day national and political denominations are misleading when applied retroactively to describe historical societal evolutions over centuries, not to speak of over millennia: both the contemporary Greek and Turkish national identities are modern constructions, dating from respectively the beginning and the end of the nineteenth century. 'Turk' is a particularly ambiguous label which is applied all too liberally to a wide variety of peoples throughout space and time, from the Ottomans to the Bosnian Muslims that Serbs and Croats still pejoratively continue to call 'Turks', to the Christian Arabs who migrated to Latin

America from the Ottoman Empire in the nineteenth century, whose descendants are even today referred to as *Turcos*. The Argentinian president in the early 1990s, Carlos Menem, was one of these and was thus called *El Turco*.

Even though Europeans have always referred to the Ottoman Empire as 'Turkey', and to the Ottomans as 'Turks', its own rulers never thought of themselves as Turks. Indeed, they were not, in the modern sense. The Ottoman founder Osman's tribe were among the Central Asian tribes that had entered Anatolia at the end of the eleventh century. The people that make up the Turkish nation today have a vast variety of ethnic origins. When the Central Asian tribes settled in Anatolia they mixed with the Byzantine-era Christian population of the peninsula. The Central Asian tribes are estimated to have added maybe 10 per cent to the Anatolian population. In the course of 150 years, the small Ottoman emirate had expanded into a world power. The Ottoman armies conquered the Balkans, rode into the old Byzantine capital Constantinople in 1453 and reached far into Europe; they were halted only at the gates of Vienna. The Black Sea became an Ottoman lake; almost the whole extent of North Africa, from Algeria to Egypt, came under Ottoman rule.

For six centuries, Osman's heirs managed to hold together a sprawling, multi-ethnic empire. Contrary to the image of wild barbarians conquering territory and imposing an unyielding 'Asiatic despotism', the Ottomans were successful because they showed tremendous adaptability. Warfare was only part of their success. Modern scholarship has revised the traditional European representation of the 'terrible Turk'.[1] The ability to absorb diverse populations and create new institutions and new elites is the hallmark of all successful empires, and the Ottomans were good students of the Byzantines they superseded. But perhaps specific to the Ottomans was their continued flexibility and adaptability. They persisted in their mode of absorption and adaptation until the nineteenth century, when they were – as we will see in more detail later – overwhelmed by the dual forces of nationalism and European capitalism.

The Ottomans quickly outgrew their tribal, ethnic origins. They mixed with and assimilated the aristocracies of the Byzantine Empire and those of the Slavic kingdoms in the Balkans which became the core region of the empire, from where its elite were drawn. The Ottoman state was a hybrid entity, an Islamic-Christian synthesis. Every single one of Osman's successors took a Christian-born wife. After the conquest of Constantinople, 'the Ottoman palace was packed with Byzantine and Balkan aristocrats'.[2] Out of the 15 Ottoman grand viziers (chief ministers) between 1453 and 1515, eight were of Byzantine or Balkan nobility, four rose to the ranks from the *devshirme* system,[3] and only three were of Muslim Turkish origin.[4] 'Turk' was used pejoratively and referred to the Muslim peasants in Anatolia; but they did not think of themselves as 'Turks' either.

This mixing at the elite level was paralleled on a popular level in Anatolia. It was not Ottoman practice to convert Christians to Islam, but by the sixteenth century, Anatolia, where the Christians (Greeks and Armenians) had formed the majority until the thirteenth century, had a Muslim majority, and the Turkic language of the immigrants from Central Asia was dominant. This was a natural process, as the populations mixed. But the rapid linguistic and religious makeover of Hellenistic Anatolia is all the more remarkable since it was not the result of a massive invasion or forced conversions. The majority of the largely Greek-speaking Anatolian peasantry abandoned its language and religion; what facilitated this was the fact that the Greek Orthodox creed was identified with an aristocratic and clerical elite, and with the church as an instrument of state oppression. The newcomers from Central Asia overthrew this political order, while adopting elements of the native popular culture. A folk religion emerged – the Alevi creed – combining elements of the pre-Islamic, shamanic faith of the tribes from Central Asia, Shiite Islam, and the Greek Orthodox folk creed of the native peasantry. This made it natural and easy for the Greek-speaking Christian Anatolian peasants to become Turkic-speaking Muslims. By the nineteenth century, 80 per cent of the population of Anatolia – nearly 10 million out of a total of little more than 12 million – was Muslim. Twenty per cent – 2.3 million – was Christian. The total population of the empire, including its territories in the Balkans, the Middle East and North Africa, was 35 million in the mid nineteenth century, with 21 million Muslims and 14 million Christians.

The language of the imperial elite, Ottoman, *Osmanlı*, was a mixture of Turkish, Persian and Arabic, and incomprehensible to the ruled. Even though it was not unusual for pre-modern ruling elites to use idioms that differed in one way or another from the languages of the people they ruled, the Ottoman imperial elite was nonetheless uniquely culturally detached from the subjects of the empire. Ottoman and Turk were not only distinct but antagonistic identities. There were several other Turkic emirates in Anatolia, and these resisted the Ottomans longer than the Christian kingdoms in the Balkans had done. While we are used to thinking of the Ottomans as easterners and 'Turks' who threatened European Christendom, for the other Turkic emirates in Anatolia the Ottomans were 'Westerners': the Ottoman army that subjugated the Turkic emirates and the Anatolian Turkish nobility that was seen as a potential rival to the Ottoman household was composed of Serbians and other Christians from the Balkans, while the Ottoman elite forces – the *janissaries* – were made up of Christians who had been converted to Islam.

Since its founding, the authoritarian Turkish nation state has rejected the diversity that the Ottomans embraced for most of their existence. But in at least one respect Turkey is the heir of the Ottoman state: while practising tolerance toward Christians and Jews, the Ottomans also established a sinister pattern of violence that, unlike their multiculturalism, has persisted to this day. Their tolerance of diversity never included Muslims who did not embrace the Sunni orthodoxy of the state, such as the heterodox Alevis. One Ottoman sultan, Selim I (1470-1520), was particularly ferocious; the slaughter of the Alevis during his reign was the first genocide in Anatolia. Alevis still remember his name with dread. And it was not a politically innocent act when in 2013 Erdoğan decreed that a new bridge over the Bosporus in Istanbul that connects Europe and Asia was to be named after the slayer of the Alevis. During the Ottoman era, many of the Alevis who survived the repeated massacres were forcefully converted to Sunni Islam, the official state religion, a practice that the Turkish state has assumed as well. More blood was spilled in Anatolia during the Ottomans' sustained, centuries-long effort to subjugate the Alevi majority than had been spilled in the Balkans, where Ottoman rule was established with relative ease.

By the end of the First World War, everything was lost. The last sultan, Mehmed VI, was a pathetic figure: he clung to the futile hope that collaboration with the victorious allies would secure the survival of what was left of the Ottoman state. A young Ottoman infantry general, one of the very few who could boast a successful record in the First World War, Mustafa Kemal, thought otherwise. Kemal, a Macedonian, would later name himself Atatürk, the 'Father Turk'. In May 1919 Kemal, who was to become Turkey's first president in 1923, left the capital Constantinople for Anatolia, where he took charge of the nationalist resistance movement and launched an insurrection against the collaborationist policies of the Ottoman government. Kemal could count on one important ally: Bolshevik Russia. The reaction in Russia to what was described as the 'Turkish Revolution' was highly favourable. It was interpreted as a counterpart and extension into the Muslim world of the Russian Revolution. *Izvestia* welcomed it as 'the first Soviet revolution in Asia'.[5] Indeed, Kemal himself provided reasons to believe that this might be the case. In an interview with the UK Labour Party's *Daily Herald* in 1922, Kemal described himself as both nationalist and socialist: 'The new Turkish idea wants to govern through a system that is not that far from socialism. I do not want to say that we are communists. We are not, because we are nationalists. Me personally, I am a socialist as far as this does not conflict with my nationalism.'[6]

Kemal had no compunction in opportunistically appealing to different ideological constituencies when political expediency so required; as well as presenting himself as a socialist, he similarly at the same time posed as a defender of the Muslim faith, and took the title *ghazi*, a holy warrior. Lenin for one hardly imagined that Kemal was a 'socialist', but he valued him as an ally against the Western imperialist powers. Lenin's government and Kemal's nationalist movement had a common enemy in Great Britain. Turkey was strategically important to the besieged Bolsheviks, and could protect their exposed flank in the Caucasus. For Kemal, securing Russian arm supplies was no less an urgent necessity. From the moment he set foot on Anatolian soil, Kemal had been intent on establishing military and diplomatic relations with the Bolsheviks. For him Bolshevik Russia was not only diplomatically a counterweight to Great Britain, France and their protégé Greece, but, more importantly, the only major source of money and supplies. Kemal succeeded in securing the help of the Bolsheviks to equip his nationalist army. On 16 March 1921, the Treaty of Moscow was signed between the governments in Ankara and Moscow. The signatories took note of 'the points in common between the movement of the Eastern peoples for national emancipation and the struggle of the workers of Russia for a new social order'.[7]

Yet the Bolshevik relation was a double-edged sword for Kemal; it risked disseminating ideas that could nurture a challenge to his tenuous position of power. The successful effort to obtain gold and weapons from Moscow had encouraged the emergence of communist sympathizers in the ranks of the Turkish nationalists, including some of Kemal's own associates. Some among the nationalist deputies in the rebel parliament that assembled in Ankara in 1920 even called for the proclamation of a communist republic, asking 'why don't we proclaim communism and thus inspire our people with a new spirit and a new enthusiasm? We've no property or riches left. So what's holding us back?'[8] Lenin's promise to emancipate the subject nationalities of the defunct tsarist empire also had an impact on opinion in Anatolia, as the

Circassians – a people from the Caucasus who had sought refuge in the Ottoman Empire from the onslaught of the Russian army in the nineteenth century – formed a significant constituency. Kemal's foreign minister, who negotiated with the Bolsheviks, was a Circassian, the son of a general in the imperial Russian army who had taken refuge in the Ottoman Empire. Circassians formed the backbone of the 'Green Army', an organization that was founded in Ankara in 1920 and that combined Islamic militancy with scraps of socialism.

On 28 December 1920, the leader of the newly founded Communist Party of Turkey (TKP), Mustafa Suphi, arrived in the eastern Anatolian city of Kars, accompanied by his wife, the party secretary Ethem Nejat and 14 other TKP officials. The TKP had been founded on 10 September 1920 in Baku, the capital of Azerbaijan. The Turkish communist leadership joined a group of Russian officials who were on a mission to set up an embassy in Ankara. The TKP mission was to end in tragedy. Suphi was the son of an Ottoman provincial governor, and had received the best possible education. He graduated from the prestigious Lycée de Galatasaray, the imperial high school in Constantinople where education was given in French, and went on to study political science in Paris. His examination thesis dealt with the 'Problems and the future of agricultural credit cooperatives'. On his return to the Ottoman capital, Suphi took up work as newspaper editor and also lectured in economics. He joined the ruling Committee of Union and Progress (CUP), better known in contemporary Europe as the party of the 'Young Turks'.

The CUP had been founded in 1889 as an underground network in opposition to the autocratic sultan Abdülhamid II. The core of the CUP was made up of junior Ottoman army officers. It was an ideologically heterogeneous organization that was initially held together by its members' shared commitment to societal and political change. On 3 July 1908, CUP members in the army engineered a revolution that proclaimed 'freedom'. Elections were held, and on 17 December 1908, the parliament was convened. It was dominated by the CUP, but it reflected the multi-ethnic composition of the empire. Of the 288 parliamentarians, 147 were Turks, 60 Arabs, 27 Albanians, 26 Greeks, 14 Armenians, 10 Slavic and 4 Jews. A year later, the CUP deposed Sultan Abdülhamid after he tried to engineer a counter-coup. The Young Turk revolution was both a military coup and a popular uprising. The revolution was led by middle-class army officers; this was logical, since the military had become the avant-garde of Ottoman modernization during the course of the nineteenth century. But at the same time, the revolution also enjoyed a popular base: it had started in the Anatolian countryside, as a peasant revolt against taxation and conscription, first among Armenians, with Turks and Arabs later joining in.

Like the Ottoman Empire itself, the CUP was torn by divisions and was pulled in many different, opposing ideological directions. Its members and sympathizers demanded change, and called for an end to autocratic rule, but they could not agree on the contents of change once the revolution had succeeded and the liberal constitution had been established. The CUP counted both liberals and socialists among its active members, and it cooperated with the Armenian nationalist party, the Dashnak. At the approach of the First World War, however, the CUP turned increasingly authoritarian and aggressively Turkish nationalist. As noted earlier, the Muslim Ottoman elite did not identify as Turkish, but as Ottoman. But the attempts by Ottoman intellectuals and some statesmen during the nineteenth century to provide a common glue for the peoples of the empire by forging a shared Ottoman identity for all of its citizens proved futile; nationalism was unstoppable among both Ottoman Christians (Greeks, Bulgarians, Armenians) and increasingly also among Ottoman Muslims (Arabs, Albanians).

Turkish was the default identity for those who were left, after everyone else among the peoples of the empire had discovered their nationality. It was in a sense appropriate that the inspiration for embracing what had until then been a despised identity – which had migrated to Anatolia a millennium earlier with nomads from Central Asia – originated with Tatar-Turkic intellectuals in Russia; it was among them that the Turkish national idea was born in the nineteenth century, and it was through them that the Ottoman Muslim intellectuals grappling with issues of identity and the question of the survival of the state discovered that they were 'Turks' in the first place.

In the First Balkan War of 1912, the Ottomans lost all of their remaining possessions in the Balkans, the heartland of the empire. Historian Eugene Rogan points out that it is hard to overstate the magnitude of the Ottoman losses between 1911 and 1913, when the empire surrendered the last of its possessions in the Balkans and in North Africa, together with millions of its subjects.[9] The devastation of these wars fed Turkish fears of physical extinction. Hundreds of thousands of Muslim refugees flooded into Anatolia from the Balkans, which brought new ethno-religious tensions and rekindled old ones. By the time of the outbreak of the First World War, the immigrant population – from the Balkans and the Caucasus – represented 40 per cent of the total population of Anatolia. The leading cadres of the CUP – all of whom were of Balkan origin and who were now de facto displaced persons with no hope of returning to their homelands, among them Mustafa Kemal, who never again saw his native city Salonika (Thessaloniki in modern Greece) – concluded that there was no future left for a multi-ethnic Ottoman state. The CUP government engaged in what it saw as a struggle for 'Turkish' ethnic survival and made preparations to carve out a safe haven, ethnically cleansed of Christians, in Anatolia, until then a neglected backyard of the empire. Interestingly, Karl Marx and Friedrich Engels had seen this coming. Sixty years earlier, they had predicted that the Ottomans would ultimately be unable to hold on to the Balkans, and that the 'Turks' were sooner or later bound to end up in 'Asia Minor and Armenia'.[10] What Marx and Engels did not foresee was the terrible human destruction that the construction of this new national homeland was going to entail.

The new Turkish national home was to be cleansed of its Christian population. The 'demographic engineering' of the CUP culminated with the Armenian genocide between 1915 and 1917, in which around 1 million Ottoman Armenians are estimated to have been killed. To this day, the government of Turkey has continued to reject the use of the term genocide, and the word incites strong, emotional reactions among Turks from all walks of society and of every ideological inclination; Turkish progressives also react against its use, even though they may accept that the Armenians were the victims of atrocities. But, as Eugene Rogan notes, the available evidence fully supports the claim that the Ottoman government was responsible for 'acts committed with the intent to destroy, in whole or in part', the Armenian community of Anatolia as a distinct national and religious group, which means that the annihilation of the Armenians conforms with the definition of genocide in the 1948 UN Convention on Genocide.[11] The Armenians, concentrated in six eastern Anatolian provinces and in the capital Constantinople, made up 20 per cent of the population of the empire; today, they make up less than 0.5 per cent of the population of Turkey. The CUP government also embarked on the creation of a national economy, enacting the first measures to replace the Christian commercial bourgeoisie with a Muslim bourgeoisie. The division between a Muslim state elite and a non-Muslim, mostly Christian (Greek and Armenian) bourgeoisie – and between the latter and the Muslim popular masses – was fateful for the Ottoman Empire. We will return to this impasse later, to see how the solution to it laid the foundations for the capitalist state of Turkey.

As Turkish nationalism gathered strength, liberal dissenters in the CUP were purged. Many were consigned to internal exile. The future founding leader of the Communist Party of Turkey was among them. But Mustafa Suphi did not stay long in the city of Sinop on the Black Sea coast of Anatolia, to where he had been deported. He escaped to Russia in 1913, but was soon interned there as an enemy alien when the First World War, which pitted the Russian and Ottoman Empires against each other, broke out. He was exiled to the Ural region. But that exile was to prove decisive, as Suphi there came into contact with Turkic, Tatar communists. His ideological itinerary was anything but linear: Suphi went from being a Young Turk nationalist to adopting Bolshevik views after the Russian Revolution. But it was an itinerary that reflected the intellectual confusions of his generation, the attempts of young minds to make sense of what were extremely volatile times, with immense societal and political upheaval. Yet there was also a consistency to Suphi's thinking: the cause of national liberation, and in particular that of the 'oppressed Eastern peoples', was a theme to which he kept returning in his writings and speeches.

A source of inspiration for Suphi was Mirsaid Sultan-Galiev, a Tatar Bolshevik whose ideas about Muslim 'national communism' appealed to Ottoman Turkish socialists. Galiev held that class divisions had not yet emerged in colonial and semi-colonial societies, and that the bulk of the populations under the yoke of imperialism could be characterized as proletarians. Ottoman Turkish socialists envisioned wedding Islam, the newly invented Turkish identity, and socialism. They often embraced communism out of nationalist motivations. As we shall see in the following, nationalism has continued to motivate the mainstream Turkish left.

In his discussions with fellow socialists, Mustafa Suphi contended that it was necessary to support the Kemalists, the Ankara government, in their fight against the imperialists, even though, as he remarked in a speech, 'they might be national-ist bigots'.[12] Indeed, the national forces that Kemal led fought not only against the European powers – Britain, France, Italy and Greece – that had occupied the capital Constantinople and parts of Anatolia, but also against Anatolia's indigenous Christians, the Armenians who had survived the genocide, and the Greeks. Suphi nonetheless believed that what he called the 'Anatolian movement' provided an opportunity to build a 'Socialist Turkey'. Kemal, though, warned Suphi in September 1920 not to entertain any illusions. In a message to Suphi, who was then still in Baku, Kemal emphasized that social changes in Turkey had to be left to the discretion of his government.[13] Suphi fatefully disregarded Kemal's warning.

Mustafa Suphi did worry that his party might be attacked by Turkish nationalists, but he was still intent on pursuing the journey into Anatolia. He turned down the suggestion of General Kazım Karabekir – the commander of the Turkish army in eastern Anatolia, who met his party in Kars – that they return to Baku. Instead, they headed toward the city of Erzurum; there, the governor refused them entry into the town and sent them to the city of Trabzon on the Black Sea coast. The governor informed Kemal of his action and that the party was going to be shipped back to Russia from Trabzon. Kemal expressed no objections in his reply, only inquiring about the size of the group and if they were all travelling together. Suphi and his companions arrived in Trabzon on 28 January 1921, the last day of their lives. The welcoming party that had gathered never got a chance to greet the communists, who were taken to the harbour by the master of the local guild of boatmen, a nationalist mobster named Yahya. Mustafa Suphi, his wife Meryem, Ethem Nejat, the party secretary, and the rest of their party were forced to board a motor launch. Suphi is said to have objected, refusing to be sent back to Russia. But the mobster Yahya and his armed men, who boarded a second launch, had in all probability received other orders. They killed the 15 communists and dumped their corpses in the Black Sea.

The murder of the entire leadership of the Communist Party of Turkey was organized and carried out by right-wing Turkish nationalists. So much is evident. But who had given the order to have them killed? Yahya, the henchman, was later conveniently liquidated. What is clear is that Mustafa Kemal had wanted the Communist Party out of the country; he had warned Suphi, and his commander on the eastern front had tried to dissuade the communists from venturing into Anatolia. Andrew Mango, the author of the most recent, major biography in English of Kemal, notes that 'Mustafa Kemal's record shows that he did his best to get rid of his opponents without bloodshed. But if they refused to submit, there were always people willing to act in line with his presumed wishes.'[14] He writes that a wink was enough, and that it probably came from local nationalist authorities. Mango is clear about Kemal's responsibility: 'Mustafa Kemal could have intervened to stop the crime, but did not do so.'[15] In 1923, Kemal told Turkish journalists that his government had stopped the Russians setting up a Communist organization: 'We applied fairly strong measures', he said.[16]

The murders of 'the fifteen' were the first political mass killing in Turkey. They established a pattern that has persisted until the present. Mustafa Suphi and his companions were the first victims of the Turkish 'deep state'. Their tragic fate was mourned in what are among the most moving lines in Turkish literature:

history
is the struggle
of the classes
1921
January 28
the Black Sea
the bourgeoisie
us
fifteen severed heads
hanging from fifteen butchers' hooks comrade
don't keep their names
in your mind
but
don't forget 28 January![17]

The author of these lines, Nazım Hikmet, Turkey's greatest poet, is the icon of the Turkish left. But to the Turkish state and to the right he is to this day an intolerable communist traitor to the fatherland. The state stripped him of his citizenship in 1959, and in 2002 the interior minister asked that the birth details of Hikmet be posthumously erased from the state records, so as to make sure that no traces would be left showing that he had ever existed as a citizen of the country.

Hikmet was born into a family of Ottoman notables, and even counted Polish nobility among his ancestry. He graduated from the Ottoman Naval School, but after being swept along by the revolutionary fervour in the wake of the Russian Revolution his life took a very different turn from what his background and education had prepared for him. Like Mustafa Suphi, who had a similar social background, Hikmet decided to explore whether the nationalist resistance movement in Anatolia could provide an opportunity for socialism. The year was 1921 and he was only 19 years old. He was a romantic communist, sporting a red scarf and doing nothing to hide his subversive views. Local nationalist authorities became suspicious and first prevented him from continuing his journey, but he finally made it to Ankara, the nationalist rebel capital, where he was introduced to Kemal himself.

The nationalist general and the young communist poet shared a birthplace, the Ottoman city of Salonika, a vibrant, cosmopolitan centre and a hub of modern ideas – nationalism, liberalism and socialism – during the final decades of the Ottoman Empire. But while Hikmet hailed from the Ottoman state aristocracy, Kemal's background was low middle class. Decades later, in Moscow in 1960, Nazım Hikmet related his meeting with Mustafa Kemal to a visiting Turkish journalist.

Kemal had asked the nervous young poet what kind of poems he wrote, Hikmet recalled: 'Are they poems with a subject?' Hikmet had replied, 'Yes, overall, they are.' Kemal was displeased: 'Overall does not suffice! In days like these, you must only write poetry that has a subject. That's what the country is in need of.'[18]

Hikmet followed the advice to write committed poetry, but committed himself not to the Turkish nationalist cause, but to that of socialism and humanism. Shortly after his meeting with Kemal, he headed to Moscow. When he returned to Turkey in 1924, Kemal had established his dictatorship. Hikmet was jailed, and spent 18 years in prison. After his release, he feared for his life, and in 1951 made a dramatic escape to the Soviet Union. Hikmet had good reason to expect the worst. A few years earlier, in 1948, another prominent Turkish left-wing writer, Sabahattin Ali – whose most famous novel, *The Madonna in Fur Coat*, has now been belatedly published in English to great critical acclaim – had been brutally murdered, his head smashed in by an agent of the Turkish secret service as he tried to escape across the Turkish border to Bulgaria.

In retrospect, the fruitless encounter in Ankara in 1921 – between the general who was to carry out a secularist-nationalist 'revolution' and the young communist poet for whom there was going to be no liberty in 'revolutionary' Turkey – illustrated the contradiction that has been at the heart of Turkish progressive thinking ever since: here were two men who were both destined to be revered by the same progressives, even though their views were in fact incompatible. Kemal and Hikmet may indeed both have sensed this, yet the misguided notion that what the nationalist general and the communist poet respectively stood for are two sides of the same, progressive coin, that nationalism and leftism somehow converge in a progressive whole, has remained an article of faith for the left in Turkey. People who count themselves as progressives regret that the two men, their two heroes, did not team up. The journalist to whom Hikmet related his fruitless encounter with Kemal deplored the fact that Hikmet was not offered the opportunity to become the 'poet of the Anatolian Revolution'.[19] But there were other leftists who offered their services to Kemal's revolution. They did so imagining that the break with 'religious obscurantism' that Kemal executed, together with what appeared to be his anti-imperialist nationalism, represented the first steps toward socialism.

CHAPTER TWO

Kemalism and the Left

The Kemalist Revolution

On 1 November 1922, the Turkish Grand National Assembly in Ankara abolished the sultanate. It had taken Mustafa Kemal a combination of persuasion and menace to have his way. In a speech to the assembly he said that the 'truth' that the Turkish nation had de facto already taken sovereignty into its own hands 'will soon find expression, but some heads may roll in the process'.[1] The last Ottoman sultan left Constantinople on board a British warship. By that time, Kemal's forces had established full control over Anatolia, and were soon also going to take control over Constantinople and eastern Thrace, the region that forms the European part of Turkey today. The invading Greek army in Anatolia was routed. On 9 September 1922, Turkish nationalist forces entered the city of Smyrna, which had a Christian majority. A terrible humanitarian tragedy ensued. Upon entering the city, the commander of the Turkish forces, Nurettin Pasha, handed over the Orthodox Archbishop Chrysostomos to a Turkish mob that proceeded to tear out the Archbishop's beard, gouge out his eyes with knives, and cut off his ears, nose and hands. For the following fortnight, Smyrna was sacked by the Turks. Thirty thousand Greeks and Armenians are estimated to have been massacred.

Much of the city, the Greek and Armenian quarters, was burnt down. The Christian majority of Smyrna was evicted.

Over a million other Greek-Orthodox Christian Anatolians were to follow them after the conclusion of the Lausanne peace treaty. The treaty was signed on 24 July 1923. It formally ended the conflict between the victorious powers of the First World War and Turkey, and delineated the borders of the new Turkish state. These borders have since only changed once, when in 1939 Turkey annexed the province of Alexandretta, which was then part of French-held Syria.

It has been said that whether we like it or not, those of us who live in Europe, or in other places influenced by European political ideas, are 'the children of Lausanne'.[2] We are so in the sense that the treaty signed beside the idyllic Swiss lake in 1923 established a baleful principle. Under the auspices of the so-called international community, the governments of Turkey and Greece agreed to exchange populations: about 400,000 Muslims were forced to move from Greece to Turkey, while at least 1.2 million Greek Orthodox Christians were either expelled from Turkey to Greece, or, if they had already been forced to flee, told that they could never again return to their homes. In his book about the mass expulsions that forged modern Greece and Turkey, Bruce Clark writes that 'for the remainder of the century, the memory of the giant Greek-Turkish exchange was a powerful influence on policy makers all over the world. It was taken as proof that it was possible, both practically and morally, to undertake huge exercises in ethnic engineering, and proclaim them a success.'[3]

The Lausanne treaty enshrined taking the easy way out as a guiding principle: disputes over territory could and should be solved by forcing everybody on the 'wrong side' of newly drawn territorial borders to move, until boundaries and ethnic groups coincided perfectly. In fact, many of the 'Greeks' who were expelled from their ancestral home were Turkish-speakers, while the Muslims from Greece were not 'Turks' ethnically. Meanwhile, those Armenians who had survived the genocide during the First World War were of course not to be allowed to return to Anatolia. The ground had been cleared for the creation of a Muslim 'Turkish' nation state: the Christian presence in Anatolia, two millennia old, had been wiped out.

On 29 October 1923, the Grand National Assembly proclaimed the Republic of Turkey and elected Mustafa Kemal as president. His election, though, was not unanimous; many members of parliament abstained from participating in the vote. Several of Kemal's close associates sensed that he was going to make himself a dictator and worried about the direction in which he was taking the country. Some of them were liberals with a deep respect for British institutions, and they had objected to the abolition of the sultanate. The liberals had argued for transforming it into a constitutional monarchy on the British model; they pleaded for tolerance, moderation and compromise. They believed that society could only be transformed in slow and patient stages, and with the involvement of the population, from the bottom upwards. Kemal disregarded them. He was to tolerate no opposition, and he soon unsentimentally purged his liberal friends and sent them into exile. Sweeping political and juridical changes ensued. In 1924, the caliphate, the central source of religious authority, was scrapped. The caliph, Abdülmecid, was taken from the imperial palace, put on a train and deported within hours. All other remaining members of the Ottoman royal family were deported. The abolition of the caliphate provoked the first, major Kurdish revolt in 1925. It took fully half of the Turkish army, more than 50,000 troops, to crush the rebellion of Sheikh Sait, a Kurdish tribal and religious leader, who was hanged. The rebellion was not motivated by ethnic nationalism, but by a conservative religiosity that remains strong to this day in the Kurdish regions of Anatolia. Yet it did nonetheless represent the first expression of an ethnic fissure that has since only continued to widen.

Although only ceremonial, the institution of the caliphate was nonetheless revered across the Muslim world and its abolition caused a wave of protests, from Egypt to India. The Indian Muslims had lent financial support to Kemal's cause, and were bitterly disappointed when he turned against Islamic institutions once he had vanquished the Western powers. In Egypt, the Muslim Brotherhood – an anti-colonial, Islamic resistance group founded in 1928, and which wanted to put an end to the British occupation of Egypt – saw the abolishment of the caliphate as part of the wider, Western imperial assault against the Muslim world, and promised to re-institute it. But it would be a mistake to make too much of the religious dimension; to this day, in the West, the Islamic caliphate conjures the image of a 'Muslim world' that is assumed to be unified, and as such to constitute a threat to the West. In fact, Muslims have never universally rallied to the caliphate. The Ottoman sultans had laid claim to the title of caliph, the leader of the *ummah*, ever since they occupied Egypt in the sixteenth century, but to little political effect. At the end of the nineteenth century though, the Ottoman sultan Abdülhamid II had made the caliphate the centrepiece of his attempt to bolster the political legitimacy of his reign. After the loss of much of the Balkans, the Ottoman Empire had become much more Muslim, and there was a political logic to accentuating the Islamic element in order to keep its different Muslim peoples, who now constituted a much larger majority, together. Abdülhamid also tried to use the caliphate to whip up international Muslim solidarity, hoping that this would help him stave off the growing threat from the Western imperial powers, but in vain. The only tangible effect that Abdülhamid's appeal to 'Islamism' had was to contribute to the fantasy of a global, Islamist conspiracy in European minds. When the Ottoman sultan-caliph declared *jihad*, holy war, upon the Ottomans' entry into the First World War, no other Muslim nation heeded the call; on the contrary, Muslim rulers and religious authorities in India and North Africa dismissed the Ottoman sultan's claim to caliphal authority and his right to declare *jihad* on behalf of the Muslim community of faithful. Indian Muslims in the British army fought against

Figure 1   The newly elected president Mustafa Kemal (in fur cap to the right of the picture), followed by his wife (in headscarf), among religious and other notables on a tour in Anatolia in 1924.

the Ottomans in Mesopotamia; and in Hejaz and in Syria, Ottoman Arab Muslims made common cause with Great Britain and revolted against the sultan-caliph.

Kemal attacked both official and popular religion: in short order, he did away with the religious courts that applied Islamic law, substituting civil law for the sharia; he abolished the separate religious schools and colleges, establishing a unified secular system of public education; he closed down shrines and suppressed the dervish orders that had been the locus of popular religiosity for centuries. He also banned the fez, which he held to be a symbol of religious traditionalism. At a diplomatic reception, Kemal even knocked the fez off the head of the Egyptian ambassador. In fact, the fez had been introduced by an early modernizer, the Ottoman sultan Mahmud II (1785-1839), who had replaced the turban with what he thought was the more European-looking fez. Kemal also changed the calendar, imposing the Gregorian system. Although the conservative historian Bernard Lewis described Kemal's rule as a 'dictatorship without the uneasy over-the-shoulder glance, the terror of the door-bell, the dark menace of the concentration camp',[4] the Kemalist 'reforms' were nonetheless enforced brutally, and protesters were hanged. What caused the most popular uproar was the 'hat reform'.

Kemal was inspired by the French Revolution, but while the French revolutionaries were backed by the peasantry when they fought the Catholic Church, the Kemalist revolution confronted the popular masses when it took on Islamic institutions. The Marxist historian Perry Anderson notes that 'the scale and the speed of this assault on religious tradition and household custom, embracing faith, time, dress, family, language, remain unique in the *ummah* to this day. No one could have guessed at such radicalism in advance. Its visionary drive separated Kemal from his predecessors with éclat.'[5] Still, Kemal was a realist; even though for him Islam and civilization may have been a contradiction in terms, and even though he perhaps ideally would have wanted to do away with the Muslim faith all together – Kinross claims that he once said of the Turks, 'If only we could make them Christians'[6] – he nonetheless recognized that Islam was an indispensable glue for the nation that he had set about to forge. When the Christian Gagauz Turks in Romania wanted to migrate to Turkey in the 1930s, they were rejected. However 'Turkish' ethnically, they had the 'wrong' faith.

Kemal's radicalism, his agnosticism and his devotion to the ideals of the European Enlightenment are usually explained with reference to his personal background: he is supposed to have been disgusted by his mother's devoutness, to have felt ridiculed by his fellow European officers' reaction to his Ottoman headgear, the fez, and to have himself been repelled by the 'Arab fanaticism'[7] he encountered on duty in Syria. The Kemalist revolution is conventionally seen as an historical anomaly, an 'idealist' endeavour that appears to have owed its realization exclusively to the personal, rationalist convictions, if not whims, of one very unique man, and thus independent of social and material conditions, as if carried out in a societal vacuum. This is mistaken, even though Kemal's personality did make a difference: he was prepared to go to much greater lengths in forcing through change than anyone else in the modernist ranks of the state and military elite. However, rationalist, secularist ideas were common currency among his generation of Ottoman officers and educated cadres. Modernization was in the air. Anderson observes that 'systematic though it was, the transformation that now gripped Turkey was a strange one: a cultural revolution without a social revolution, something historically very rare, indeed that might look a priori impossible. The structure of society, the rules of property, the pattern of class relations, remained unaltered.'[8] In fact, in Anatolia, class divisions were not deep; except for in the Kurdish, tribal areas in the south-east, feudalism did not hold sway. The Ottomans had not permitted the emergence of a powerful landowning class in the Anatolian countryside. Peasant holdings prevailed.

The landholding pattern in Anatolia had kindled the interest of none other than Karl Marx. Marx's universalism, which found its classic expression in the *Communist Manifesto*, instructed that all nations must submit to the forces of bourgeois modernity; this left little room for the possibility of independent revolution in less developed regions around the globe. In this vein, Marx celebrated the dissolution of the archaic village system in India under British rule. However, partly because the failure of the Paris Commune in 1871 led him to despair about the prospects for a communist revolution in Europe, Marx became more open to the possibility of revolution in those parts of the globe where capitalism had not yet developed. He was especially interested in Russia, but what is less well known is that he also developed an interest in the conditions in the Ottoman Empire. As Marx explored whether the Russian village commune could offer a foundation for socialism, he developed a parallel interest in the Anatolian peasantry, so much so that he even decided to study Turkish while also learning Russian. These studies late in his life came to naught. Marx never acquired any deeper knowledge about what he imagined was a village commune in Anatolia. But he had a hunch: what is interesting is that Marx entertained the hope that the 'Turkish' – as he called it – peasantry held the key to the democratization of the authoritarian order. A century later, the Turkish social democratic leader Bülent Ecevit, to whom we will return, thought along similar lines, and he picked up and fleshed out Marx's idea when he promoted the 'village-city' as the agent of economic development and the political emancipation of the peasantry.

Anderson remarks that the fact that there was little or no class conflict to contain or suppress meant that the Kemalist regime could dispense with popular mobilization: Kemal did not stage mass rallies, bombard the nation with speeches or organize spectacular processions or parades. Historians usually make the point that Kemalist Turkey differed from the fascist regimes of Germany and Italy because it lacked the crucial ingredients of 'charismatic rule' and mass mobilization. No Nuremberg-style rallies were held in Anatolia. Yet admiring fascist commentators in Europe at the time saw things differently: Atatürk did not need to mobilize the masses, they pointed out, because he had already secured their allegiance by defeating foreign enemies. Fascists across Europe in the 1930s did not think that fascism depended on 'charismatic rule' and mass mobilization. Fascist Italy's foreign minister used Atatürk's example to predict what might become of General Francisco Franco if he were to emerge victorious from the civil war in Spain: 'If Franco wins militarily, he will have the necessary prestige required to govern just as Kemal Pasha lived for twenty years on the undisputed merit of having liberated the country with arms.'[9] At first glance, the parallel between Kemal and Franco seems out of place. Kemal had defeated foreign enemies, emerging victorious from what Turkish historiography calls the Turkish War of Independence. This is also how international scholarship has routinely come to refer to the war. Yet, as I pointed out in the first chapter, the war in Anatolia between 1919 and 1923 was fought not only against foreign troops – against the Greek army that had occupied western Anatolia and the French who laid claim to the region of Cilicia in southern Anatolia – it was as much, if not more so, a civil war, fought against the indigenous, Christian population of Anatolia. It would be more accurate to refer to it as the Anatolian war, which accounts for both facets of the war. Kemal could indeed govern on the undisputed merit of having liberated the country from foreign troops, but he was also, like Franco, the victor of a civil war.

At a superficial glance, Kemal's revolution was, as Anderson writes, a strange one, seemingly without a social or class dimension and not sustained by a dynamic of class struggle. The Kemalist regime did not have to deal with any major class challenge, except when a wave of strikes among the small working class in Istanbul in the early 1920s was repressed. Eventually, however, the pattern of class relations was to be altered when industrialization in the decades that followed after Kemal turned increasing numbers of peasants into an industrial working class, leading to class conflict. Later, when we look at Turkey's capitalist development, it will become clear that Kemal's cultural 'reforms' in fact did have a class aspect, as they were the expressions of a bourgeois radicalism. It was not a coincidence that the Kemalist regime was pitiless in its persecution of leftists. Yet, despite what had been done to its leadership, the banned Communist Party of Turkey continued to see a revolutionary potential in Kemalism. The 1920s were dire times for the TKP as it tried to recover after the annihilation of its leadership. The party reorganized as an underground force, electing a new secretary-general, Şefik Hüsnü, at a secret meeting in Istanbul in 1925. Hüsnü did not expect to see a popular revolution in Turkey; in his writings he acknowledged that there were no objective conditions for any social mass uprising in Turkey. Since the peasants owned their land, class divisions in the Anatolian countryside were thus nowhere as deep as they were in, for example, China. Industry was underdeveloped and the working class was exceptionally weak. But the leader of the Communist Party of Turkey nonetheless deplored the fact that the Kemalist revolution had not been completed with social and political reforms in the interest of the popular masses.

The stance of the Soviet Communist Party toward Kemalist Turkey remained conditioned by its desire to maintain the friendly relations that had been established in order to counter Western imperialism. However, there were those within the TKP who deviated from this stance; at the sixth congress of the Communist International in 1928, the TKP delegate objected to the official report on Turkey that recommended continued support for Mustafa Kemal, who was described as a progressive anti-imperialist. Yet, at the end of the day, the TKP came down on the side of Kemalism and exonerated its repression. The communists endorsed Kemalism as an anti-imperialist and anti-feudal bourgeois revolutionary force. In this vein, the TKP excused the oppression of the Kurds. When the Kurds rebelled in 1925, led by the religious leader Sheikh Sait, the rebellion was denounced as a 'religious, reactionary uprising'.[10] As noted above, the rebellion was indeed religiously motivated, triggered by the abolition of the caliphate, but the Kurdish rebels were also accused of serving the interests of imperialism, of being a fifth column for British imperialism. At the time, Turkey and Great Britain were locked in a diplomatic conflict over the Mosul region in British-occupied Iraq, and British agents may indeed have incited the Kurdish tribes to rebel to divert Turkish attention to the home front.

During the 1930s, the TKP leader Şefik Hüsnü was to grow increasingly disappointed with Kemalism. In a speech at the Communist International in 1934, he described Kemalist Turkey as a 'violently oppressive terror regime'.[11] Indeed, by the 1930s, Kemal's Republican People's Party (CHP) had come under the spell of fascism. In 1936, the general secretary of the CHP, Recep Peker, was dispatched on a mission to Italy to conduct a closer study of the fascist regime there. Impressed by what he saw, upon his return Peker submitted a proposal to reorganize the Turkish regime according to fascist principles. İsmet İnönü, the prime minister, had no objections and approved the fascist blueprint, sending it on to the president for final approval. Atatürk, though, was disgusted. He spent a whole night reading the blueprint, after which he dismissed Peker as party general secretary. The incident also made him question the judgement of his prime minister, who had been his closest collaborator for many years. Atatürk wondered if İnönü was in the habit of signing documents without having read them. Atatürk had nothing but contempt for Mussolini and Hitler. However, modern scholarship has revealed that the Nazis themselves held 'The Turkish Führer', as they referred to him, and what they called the 'Turkish model', in the highest esteem.[12] Hitler said that Kemal had been a 'shining star for him',[13] and continued to express deep admiration for the Turkish leader until the end of his life. Atatürk, according to Hitler, was the first to show that it is possible to regenerate and mobilize the resources a country has lost: 'In this respect Atatürk was a teacher; Mussolini was his first and I his second student.'[14] A formidable Atatürk cult developed in Germany during the Nazi years. Time and again the Nazi press affirmed that Atatürk's revolution had been *the* national revolution, and that Turkey had shown the way by how it dealt with its minorities. Hitler also admired the resolve Atatürk had demonstrated in his fight against 'the church': 'How fast Kemal Atatürk dealt with his priests is one of the most amazing chapters (of history)', he remarked.[15]

The admiration of the Nazis was unreciprocated, yet their Atatürk cult – which has been brought to light by the German historian Stefan Ihrig, whose ground-breaking study I have been referring to – is not inconsequential for how we evaluate the nature of Kemalism. The admiration of the Nazis does not in itself make Kemalism fascist, but it is nonetheless worth reflecting on why they identified themselves with the Kemalists. As the Nazis saw it, one precondition for Atatürk's success was the prior destruction of the Armenians. Indeed, many years later, in 2008, a Turkish minister of defence endorsed this view when he asked rhetorically if Turkey would ever have been a national state had the Greeks remained in the Aegean region and had there still been Armenians in many parts of the country. The question of race was central to the Nazi vision of Atatürk's success. There was nothing coincidental about their frequent attribution of the quality '*völkisch*' to the New Turkey. Ihrig writes that '"From the mishmash of peoples to völkisch purity and a vibrant and potent new state" could have been the by-line to all the Nazi narratives of the New Turkey.'[16] What matters more than the fact that Kemal despised the Nazis is that he was as obsessed as they were with 'national purity'. Mass deportations, executions and systematic Turkification were defining features of Kemal's regime, and the repression grew more severe during the 1930s. Although Kemal resisted full identification with fascist regimes – 'I want to create a liberal republic',[17] he once said – Turkey was nonetheless pulled into the orbit of fascism. During the Second World War, under his successor İnönü, the fascist traits of the regime became increasingly pronounced.

In 1937, the Alevi Kurds in the eastern Dersim region rose in revolt. Atatürk showed no pity, and ordered it crushed. Tens of thousands were killed as modern weapons of destruction, bombers, heavy artillery and gas were deployed in the massacres of the civilian population. Atatürk – who was by then terminally sick with cirrhosis of the liver, caused by his lifelong heavy drinking – travelled to the war zone to personally supervise the onslaught. It was during this war against the people of Dersim that the world's first female fighter pilot presented herself: Sabiha Gökçen was a survivor of the Armenian genocide whom Kemal had come across at an orphanage and adopted. Gökçen's Armenian origin was unknown to the Turkish public until the Armenian-Turkish journalist Hrant Dink revealed it. Dink caused an uproar with his revelation. Turkish extreme nationalists accused him of having defamed a national hero, and he was indicted for having insulted Turkishness. Dink was assassinated outside the offices of his Turkish-Armenian newspaper, *Agos*, on 19 January 2007. He was shot in the back of the head. The message was immediately clear: revenge had been avenged. The mastermind of the Armenian genocide during the First World War, the Ottoman interior minister and one of the triumvirs of the ruling CUP,

Talat Pasha, had been assassinated in the same way in Berlin in 1921 by an Armenian militant.

Dink's assassination had all the hallmarks of an operation of the Turkish 'deep state' described in the first chapter. The assassin, an adolescent of a socially destitute background, was apprehended, but it was obvious that he had not acted on his own. The complicity of the usual suspects – the right-wing nationalist assassination networks within the security services, the police and gendarmerie – was evident. But as usual, no effort was made to bring those who were responsible to justice. The police did not even bother to hide their involvement; the arresting police officers had themselves filmed together with the assassin, proudly holding up a Turkish flag with him. Dink had the typical profile of a victim of the Turkish deep state: he was a member of an ethnic minority in addition to being a socialist. Tens of thousands of Turks demonstrated on the day of Dink's funeral, holding up boards with the text 'We are all Armenians'. It was a unique manifestation of Turkish solidarity with the Armenians, and it encouraged many liberal and leftist Turkish intellectuals to think that their society was finally coming to terms with its dark past. That was prematurely optimistic. The path that Turkey has to travel remains a long one. The assassination of Dink demonstrated the resilience of the poisonous notion of '*völkisch* purity' that Kemalism introduced, and which it shared with its fascist contemporaries in the Europe of the 1920s and 1930s.

The Turkish left has by and large remained beholden to Kemalist nationalism as an expression of 'anti-imperialism'. Kemal did upset the designs of European imperialists, but what was infinitely more consequential was that the Anatolian war resulted in the ethnic cleansing of the Greek-Orthodox population of Anatolia and that the return of the Armenians who had survived the genocide was prevented. Once victory was secured, Kemal moved to mend fences with the Western imperialists: Western capital was invited to invest in Turkey and Kemal personally took charge of nurturing close relations with the leaders of Great Britain and the United States, exchanging letters with President Franklin Delano Roosevelt and hosting King Edward VIII in Istanbul. Atatürk had no appetite for shouldering the role of leader of the 'cause of the East' against European imperialism, as the leftist supporters of his regime encouraged him to do. When the Cold War broke out, Turkey joined the Western alliance, becoming a member of NATO in 1952. Turkish leftists have since held that this was a break with and a betrayal of Kemal's supposed anti-imperialism; in fact, Atatürk had always been pro-Western, and, contrary to what the left imagines, his successors have remained faithful to his legacy.

The supposedly 'anti-imperialist' origin of Turkish nationalism has bequeathed the left a disorienting legacy: we saw that the Communist Party of Turkey endorsed the brutal repression of the first Kurdish rebellion in 1925, partly because the rebels were seen to be agents of imperialism, and partly because their motives were religious. The stance of socialists and communists on the Kurdish issue has changed totally since those early days of the republic, but the mainstream of the Turkish left – secularist-nationalists and social democrats – has remained under the spell of Kemal's nationalism: such leftists have historically endorsed the forced assimilation of the Kurds, and they have continued to deny the Armenian genocide.

Kemalism has imposed a circumscribed self-definition of the left: Turkish progressives remain beholden to Kemalism and have given priority to fighting what they have taken to be 'religious obscurantism'. That fight has meant much more to them than fighting social injustice. The left has taken issue with religion, and much less, if at all, with capitalism. No wonder that the popular appeal of the left has been limited. This did not change until the late 1960s, with the rise of populist social democracy, to which we will turn our attention later. But be they social democrats, socialists or communists, Turkish leftists – with the exception of the liberal leftists whose acquaintance we will soon make – share the belief that the Kemalist revolution was 'enlightened', and that the secularist-nationalist founding ideology of Turkey – although deeply anti-democratic – nonetheless provides a basis for leftist politics.

The Kemalist Left

Kemal had aspired to modernize Turkey, to elevate the country to, as he put it, the level of 'contemporary civilization'. Since then, Kemalist leftists have remained preoccupied by one simple question: 'Why is Turkey backward?' They have held 'religious obscurantism' and imperialism responsible for the country's social, economic and, not least for what they have taken to be, cultural underdevelopment. And they have called for building on Kemal's cultural and educational reformism with economic reforms that would provide the first step toward socialism. The main theorist of this Kemalist left was a French-educated social scientist, Doğan Avcıoğlu, who became the towering figure of intellectual life in Turkey during the 1960s. He argued that Turkey's development and social justice required it to free itself from the yoke of American imperialism and adopt a statist, planned economy. It was the state bureaucracy, not the popular masses, that were going to be empowered. The Kemalist left stressed secularism, the fight against the 'religious reactionaries'. It had very much in common with the state socialism of the Ba'ath Party dictatorships in Turkey's southern neighbours Syria and Iraq. Avcıoğlu's books had a wide audience, not least among the officers' corps. The 1960s was a decade when industrialization, which had started to gather steam during the 1950s, altered the patterns of conflict in Turkish politics: the growth of the working class was starting to have a political impact. The socialist Labour Party of Turkey (TİP) entered parliament with 15 lawmakers after the general election in 1965, in which it received 3 per cent of the votes. This is to date the only time that a socialist party has gained representation in the Turkish parliament. But what was more consequential was that the Republican People's Party – the party founded by Kemal, and which had held the reins of power until it lost the first free election, held in 1950 – began to reposition itself as a centre-left party. We will be looking more closely at the emergence of populist social democracy in the following.

However, it was not the people that the Kemalist left sought to mobilize for their cause. It was the military. A Kemalist leftist intellectual avant-garde had coalesced around Avcıoğlu and the political journal *Yön* ('Direction'), which he edited. These intellectuals did not think that the revolution could be carried out by the working class; the workers were still too few, and uneducated. Instead, the 'national revolution' – a term coined by Avcıoğlu, though he also used the term 'leftist nationalist' to describe his political programme – was to be entrusted the military. The Kemalist left had reason to feel hopeful about the prospects of a left-wing military takeover. There was a strong progressive faction within the military, and plans were hatched for a leftist coup that was scheduled to take place on 9 March 1971. A 'revolutionary constitution' was drafted; the blueprint emphasized social justice but called for restricting democratic liberties. Turkey was to embark on a 'non-capitalist road to development'. An earlier military coup had already showed the way. On 27 May 1960, a group of junior officers had overthrown the government of the conservative Democratic Party (DP) in Turkey's first coup. The deposed prime minister, Adnan Menderes, and the foreign and finance ministers, were hanged a year later. Although the 1960 coup set a terrible precedent for the future, its short-term consequences were paradoxically beneficial for the left. As we will see later, in Chapter 4, the deposed conservatives had turned increasingly authoritarian, and broad sections of Turkish society clamoured for freedom. A new constitution was enacted in 1961 and democratic rule was restored. In 1963 workers were accorded the right to organize trade unions, which gave them collective bargaining rights and legalized strikes.

At first, the Kemalist leftist coup planned for March 1971 enjoyed the support of the army and air force commanders. However, the generals and others in the higher military echelons grew increasingly wary of the leftist ideological tilt of the conspirators, and at the last moment switched their loyalties. They conspired to delay the left-wing coup, and instead engineer a right-wing counter-coup. This took place on 12 March 1971. Ostensibly, the coup targeted the conservative prime minister, the leader of the Justice Party (AP), Süleyman Demirel, who was forced to resign. This helped to establish the myth according to which Turkey is authoritarian because the military does not respect civilian rule. In reality, the coup makers and the deposed government shared the same right-wing ideology. The socialist Labour Party was banned. Leftist activists were jailed. Three were executed. Kemalist leftists in the military were purged. The conspirators of the originally scheduled 'state socialist' coup were all retired from the military, and their leaders were arrested, including the ideologue of the Kemalist left, Doğan Avcıoğlu. He was tortured; after his release, he retreated to his study and devoted his last remaining years – he died prematurely of cancer in 1983 – to writing a multivolume history of the Turkic peoples inspired by the French Annales school.

The Kemalist leftist coup was derailed, but it had come close to succeeding. Ultimately, however, the notion that Turkey, a crucial NATO country that bordered the Soviet Union, could or would be allowed to liberate itself from the bonds of Western imperialism as the conspirators had ambitioned, was always unrealistic. This was also the reason why the high command intervened. The Turkish generals knew well not to challenge the United States. Since 1971, the Turkish officers' corps has been free from anything that smacks of the left; social democrats were no longer accepted as officers. That year marked the starting point of a process that was to culminate in the failed coup of 15 July 2016, which demonstrated that members of a conservative religious fraternity, the so-called Gülenists, to whom we will return, had become entrenched in the military. Starting in the 1970s, the military, in spite of officially paying lip service to secularism, took to promoting religious conservatism in order to counter the left. The Turkish military is the watchdog, not of secularism, but of the bourgeois order of the country.

But the Kemalist left was defeated not only because it had run up against forces – the military hierarchy, Turkey's NATO ties – that were too powerful; what doomed it was also its isolation from the people, which was itself a consequence of its resentment of democracy. The tragedy of the Kemalist leftists is their distrust of the people, and their contemptuous view of democracy. In elitist vein, they have held the ordinary people of Turkey to be too unsophisticated and uneducated to make proper use of democratic liberties, and that as such democracy was bound to serve only the right-wing forces who know well how to cultivate the religious feelings of the masses. Avcıoğlu's mantle was shouldered by İlhan Selçuk, his close collaborator. Selçuk was also arrested for his involvement in the leftist coup plot of 1971, and he was tortured by the military. He later became the publisher of *Cumhuriyet*, Turkey's oldest daily and the flagship of the Kemalist left, founded in 1924 – its name, which means 'republic', was chosen by Kemal Atatürk himself. To the end of his life – he died in 2010 – Selçuk remained the pre-eminent voice of the Kemalist left; to his admirers, he personified the 'Turkish Enlightenment', the Kemalist revolution. But he also personified the tragedy of the Kemalist left: the fundamental contradiction that lies at the heart of a movement that aspires to represent 'enlightenment' yet at the same time espouses a nationalism that is anything but enlightened.

Selçuk was born in 1925, to parents who were Muslim refugees from Crete. The Muslim population had been driven away from the island by the Greek nationalists at the end of the nineteenth and beginning of the twentieth century. Like most other Cretan refugees, the Selçuks were Greek-speaking, but of Muslim faith. They had spoken Greek among themselves, until the Kemalist regime in the 1930s decreed that citizens must speak only Turkish. 'My parents were scared', Selçuk recalled. He regretted that this had deprived him of a mother tongue that, he said, would have given him access to the Greek classics that inspired Enlightenment thinking. This, however, was said in private.[18] In public, Selçuk never referred to his family background nor did he ever voice any such iconoclastic, critical views of the nationalism that Atatürk imposed; instead, he kept his background a closely guarded secret and he did not allow his personal experience to colour his politics. Thus, he steadfastly opposed the Kurds' demands for linguistic and cultural freedom. In his view, democracy – in the Turkish context – was an obstacle to socialism: this was grounded in a deeply pessimistic conviction: he lamented that 'in the Muslim geography, it is always the religious reactionaries who win the elections'.

Selçuk belittlingly referred to democracy as *cici demokrasi*, 'sweet democracy'; democracy was too 'sweet' for the uneducated masses to enjoy. The popular masses could be trusted to always make the 'wrong' choice, to vote for conservatives and Islamists. Although he was tortured when he was arrested after the aborted left-wing coup in 1971, Selçuk still did not lose his illusions about the Turkish military as a vestige of 'enlightenment'. At the end of his life, he was still desperately clinging to the vain hope that the military was going to step in, overthrow Erdoğan and save 'secularism'. And even though he was strongly anti-American, Selçuk nonetheless hoped that the West would come to the rescue of secularism in Turkey. The West must be told, he said, that the 'threat against it' will not disappear until 'Islam has been exposed to enlightenment'. He believed that the American neoconservatives, people like Dick Cheney, vice president to

George W. Bush, should be courted and persuaded to make common cause against Erdoğan, who had been honoured with an invitation to the White House in 2002, even before he had been elected prime minister. Once again vainly and against political reason, as when he believed that the military was going to save secularism, Selçuk even went so far as to advocate an alliance between the secularist-nationalist left and the ultranationalist right against the Islamists. He stated that he had forgiven the far right for its violence against the left in the 1970s, but his embrace was not reciprocated: in the eyes of the far right, people like Selçuk remained hated communists.

Yet as shocking and miserable as İlhan Selçuk's embrace in late life of the far right was, it nonetheless had certain logic to it: it spoke of the ideological common ground that the Kemalist left shares with the right. Notwithstanding its pretentions to be progressive, the nationalism of the Kemalist left also has a xenophobic trait, although it is grounded in anti-capitalism and anti-imperialism, and not, as in the case of the right, in religious and cultural resentment of non-Muslims and non-Turks. This is an unfortunate consequence of the fact that Ottoman Christians and Jews came to be seen as agents of imperialism and capitalism. In the next chapter, we will take a closer look at how socioeconomic developments and ethno-religious divides in the Ottoman Empire became unfortunately intertwined during its final century. The writings of Doğan Avcıoğlu have had a profound and lasting impact on leftist thinking in this regard. He argued that the Ottoman Empire had had the potential to develop into an advanced economy by its own devices, but that it was crippled by the attack of European capitalism, and its Trojan horse, the Christians, and reduced to a semi-colonial state. According to Avcıoğlu, Turkey was disadvantaged by its geographic proximity to Europe, and stood no chance of repeating Japan's success. Indeed, the Ottoman government had been forced to sign a free trade treaty with Great Britain in 1838, which turned its land into an open market for European goods and which devastated its own manufactures. Avcıoğlu deplored the fact that the Ottoman government, under European pressure, was forced to declare all subjects, regardless of their ethnicity and creed, equal in a reform edict that was announced one year after the free trade treaty had been imposed: 'This ensured that the Greeks and Armenians on whom Western capitalism wanted to rely in Turkey were accorded a privileged position.'[19] In fact, the vast majority of the Ottoman Christians were peasants, not the *compradors*, the commercial agents in the service of European capitalism, that the Kemalist left has held them to be. In its most extreme expression, this view leads to justifying the genocide of the Ottoman Armenians during the First World War. The memoir of Şevket Süreyya Aydemir, another leading representative of the Kemalist left, offers an example.

Aydemir made the usual ideological journey of the educated of his generation: he was a Young Turk before turning to communism, and then to Kemalism. He fought against the Russians in the First World War in eastern Anatolia, and later ended up in revolutionary Russia, where he joined the Communist Party. He became a leading member of the Communist Party of Turkey but left it after a prison stint in Turkey in the 1920s. In the 1930s, Aydemir edited a political periodical, *Kadro* (The Cadre), which sought to provide arguments for developing Kemalism in a leftist direction. The regime tolerated the *Kadro* for a while, but eventually ordered it closed down. In a striking passage in his memoirs, Aydemir gives a chilling glimpse of the carnage he witnessed in Anatolia between 1915 to 1917, and offers the typical excuse for what was done to the Armenians. He writes that the Armenians had stupidly heeded the calls of the nationalist hotheads among them, when they had every reason to be contented with their lot as a 'rich bourgeoisie': 'It is a fact that the Armenians, just like all the Christian minorities in the Ottoman Empire, lived comfortable lives. They owned all commerce and business, and they were exempt from military service. They constituted the richest and thus in this respect the privileged section of the country. ... Internal as well as external trade was in their hands.'[20] While in Moscow, Aydemir made the acquaintance of the communist poet Nazım Hikmet, but he failed to heed the words of Hikmet's poem:

> The grocer Karabet's lights are on,
> This Armenian citizen has not forgiven
> the slaughter of his father in the Kurdish mountains.
> But he loves you,
> because you also won't forgive
> those who blackened the name of the Turkish people[21]

It was best, Aydemir wrote, not to seek any answers as to why the carnage had taken place; this was a page of human history that was better confined to oblivion. Turkey has indeed tried hard to pretend that the genocide did not occur. Liberal and leftist Turkish intellectuals have in recent years identified the Armenian genocide as the Turkish nation state's foundational act of violence, and argued that its denial is the main obstacle to the country's democratization. The fact that the perpetrators escaped punishment and that their acts were whitewashed has ruined the moral fabric of society. Taner Akçam – a left-wing Turkish intellectual who has done more than anyone else in his country to help it confront the crime against humanity that the Ottoman Turks committed – has pointed out that the Armenian genocide is the 'collective secret' of Turkish society, that since the founding of the republic, everyone, rightists and leftists, Muslims, Alevis, Kurds and Turks, have acquiesced in sustaining a collective 'coalition of silence'. Akçam argues that this effort is existentially rooted: 'Our existence – that of Turkey and many of its inhabitants – requires the absence of another entity: the Christians. To accept "1915" means accepting that Christians lived in this land, which almost amounts to proclaiming our own non-existence, because our existence is based on their absence, or disappearance.'[22] And even though the Turkish state has continued to vehemently deny the genocide, it has in fact appropriated it, maintaining the policy of extra-legal violence against those who are deemed to be threats to the state and the nation: the left, the Kurds and the Alevis.

Antithesis: The Liberal Left

To the Kemalist left, the state is the solution: it is endowed with the mission to 'enlighten' the uneducated masses, to liberate them from 'religious superstition', and with ensuring social justice by means of a planned economy. In the 1960s, the left's devotion to Kemalism triggered a reaction that gave birth to a liberal left, and this left has since the end of the 1980s enjoyed intellectual hegemony within the left-wing intelligentsia of the country. The socialist monthly *Birikim* (Accumulation) and the publishing house İletişim (Communication) have been the nodes of a rich, intellectual production that has deconstructed the Kemalist leftist ideological edifice. It has promoted the concept of civil society, showing that nationalism and statism are antithetical to a free society. In this sense, the liberal left has done the cause of freedom an important service. But just as the Kemalist left's embrace of state authoritarianism and nationalism – notwithstanding its progressive ambitions – made it an accomplice of the right, so has the liberal left's well-intentioned, democratic anti-statism carried the intellectuals of Turkey's 'new left' to the right: they have embraced the capitalist class as the supposed counter-force to the authoritarianism of the state. But the emergence of this liberal left also fits into an international pattern, and the timing of its rise was not coincidental.

In 1980, the socialist, communist and social democratic lefts in Turkey were crushed when the military took power and established a brutally oppressive dictatorship. We will look in more detail at how this happened in Chapter 6. The Turkish generals put in place a neoliberal economic order, just like General Augusto Pinochet had done in Chile after the overthrow of Salvador Allende in 1973. With Ronald Reagan and Margaret Thatcher neoliberalism became hegemonic in the Western world. Social democratic parties across Western Europe abandoned Keynesianism and the working class, embraced neoliberalism and globalization, and refashioned themselves as parties of the globalized middle class. With the fall of the Soviet Union, the notion that there could be any viable alternative to capitalism appeared to have been confined to the dustbin of history. If not 'the end of history', it certainly seemed to be 'the end of the left'.

It was against the background of this wider, international and ideological context of liberal ascendancy that Turkish leftist intellectuals reinterpreted the meaning of the left. Not only did the left appear dead, killed off by the 'irresistible' forces unleashed by neoliberal globalization, with military juntas assisting on occasion; to many leftist intellectuals in Turkey, the historical experience of their own country suggested that the left itself was an obstacle to democracy. This was so because, as we have seen, a Kemalist, nationalist-authoritarian interpretation of leftism had dominated what passed for the left. Turkey's liberal left was born out of this frustration with Kemalism and with its leftist avatar. The liberal dissenters have therefore been more interested in revealing the anti-democratic character of the Kemalist left than they have been in scrutinizing the authoritarianism of the hegemonic right; indeed, they mistook conservatives for the 'democratic' antithesis of the Kemalist left.

As we have seen, in the 1960s Kemalist leftists were preparing to seize power. But critical voices were raised from within the socialist Labour Party against leftist intellectuals who were busy hatching coup plans with like-minded military officers. The revolution should not be imposed from above, by the military, they objected. The leader of the Labour Party was Mehmet Ali Aybar. He was a good-humoured man, known as the politician who introduced 'socialism with a smiling face' in Turkey. Aybar coined the term that many leftists believe captures the root cause of Turkey's ills: 'the tyrannical state', in Turkish: *ceberrut devlet*. Aybar took issue both with Kemalism and with classical Marxism: he identified the state as the root of Turkey's ills, and rejected the classical class analysis of Marxism. He argued that the concepts of traditional Marxism did not apply to Turkey: unlike in the West, it was not the bourgeoisie, but the civilian-military bureaucracy that was the ruling class in Turkey. According to Aybar, the military and the bureaucrats formed 'the class that owns the state'. The state was autonomous, pursuing its own agenda independent of other economic and class interests in society. While the Kemalist left was preoccupied with Turkey's cultural and economic underdevelopment and contemptuous of 'sweet democracy', the liberal left shifted the focus to the lack of freedom. Democratic development had eluded Turkey because an octopus-like state had been controlling all walks of society since the inception of the republic and had stifled civil society. The ideological blueprint for liberal leftism was developed by an economist who was a member of the leadership of the Labour Party, İdris Küçükömer. In 1969, he published a ground-breaking book that became the cornerstone of intellectual life in Turkey and which has had a deep and lasting political impact by redefining the meaning and the purpose of the left. It was titled *Alienation of the System*. The treatise asked why democracy had eluded Turkey and, in the spirit of Aybar, identified the bureaucratic-despotic state as the culprit. The mainspring of this model is the dialectic between the state and civil society: the despotic state was held to have prevented civil society from developing and expressing itself, and had thereby disabled a democratic evolution. In fact, what liberal leftist thinking has accomplished is to have legitimized the rise of Islamic conservatism. The liberal left has provided intellectual credibility and legitimacy to the claims of the right to represent the 'people' and 'democracy' against the 'Westernizing authoritarian state elite'.

Küçükömer redefined the progressives as the 'right' and the conservatives as the 'left'. The left was undemocratic, while the right was intrinsically democratic. The pro-state progressives were not of the left as they had always imagined themselves to be; they were 'rightists' since they did not respect freedom and the autonomy of civil society. It was instead the right, the conservative parties, who were the real 'left', since they spoke for the popular masses. What had passed for the 'left' had for the last two centuries looked down on and despised the pious, conservative masses and had sought to impose its modernist values on them. The title of the book conjured up the ideological and politico-administrative elite's alienation from the culture of the popular masses. The right was the authentic 'left' because it represented the popular resentment against a tyrannically 'Westernizing' state, and it offered a democratic hope because its victory would by definition amount to the victory of civil society over the authoritarian state.

The notion of alienation has traditionally occupied a central place in the rhetoric of the Turkish right. Erdoğan has been fond of reciting these famous lines from the ultraconservative poet and ideologue Necip Fazıl Kısakürek, which evoke the sense of alienation among the popular masses which a top-down 'Westernization' of Turkish culture has supposedly caused:

You are a stranger in your homeland
a pariah in your own homeland

The Turkish right has built and sustained its hegemony by manufacturing a false political antagonism between what has been described as 'the silent Muslim majority' and 'the Westernizing state elite'. This thought figure has obscured the class dynamics at work and the class interests the right has privileged. Incongruously putting their faith in the right as a force of democracy, the liberal left has overlooked the right's authoritarian record in power; they have even provided excuses for right-wing authoritarianism. Ahmet İnsel is one of Turkey's prominent intellectuals; a self-professed socialist and a typical representative of the idiosyncratic liberal left. He explained – and excused – Erdoğan's power ambitions: Erdoğan, like other conservatives before him, needed to neutralize the Kemalist state establishment, İnsel wrote: 'They [the right] wanted to have this system [a presidential system] because they needed to mobilize the support of the sociological majority of society in order to be able to prevail against the secularist and author-itarian military-civilian bloc led by the officers. Until the AKP came to power, the Turkish right was repeatedly beaten up by this bloc.'[23]

This is a preposterously false assertion: it is the left and not the right that has been beaten up in Turkey. How do we explain the idiosyncrasy of the liberal left? It all boils down to the question of the bourgeoisie, to whether or not it is an agent of freedom, and to its relation to the state. The liberal left holds the bourgeoisie – the capitalist class, the businessmen and the industrialists – to be 'subjugated' by the despotic-bureaucratic state and maintains that it has historically been both unable and unwilling to influence politics: 'It is impossible to talk about either the political or cultural supremacy of the bourgeoisie in Turkey. The big capitalists are politically mute',[24] writes İnsel. Yet we will later see how business interests interfered in politics to bring down the social democratic leader Bülent Ecevit in the late 1970s. But the liberal left argues that the Turkish state has maintained its absolutism because there has been no strong bourgeois class to demand civil and political rights. The business class would have been 'the natural supporter of the liberal current in Turkey' had it not been for its dependency on the state for capital accumulation: '"The private initiative" does not have the historical-societal autonomy that it needs to be able to engage in a struggle with the state.'[25] The capitalist class in Turkey does owe its existence and wealth to the policies of the state, as we will see in the next chapter. But the dependency of capital on the state does not invalidate the notion of bourgeois supremacy. The capitalists may be – or appear to be – 'politically mute', but they nonetheless still rule.

In *The Eighteenth Brumaire of Louis Bonaparte* – his classic text on the question of the autonomy of the state, which remains a beacon to the debate on the relation between the state and society – Karl Marx observed that the bourgeoisie of France had seen fit to sacrifice its political liberties to secure its class interests when it bowed before the might of the state, in the person of Louis Bonaparte, who staged a coup d'état in 1851 and subsequently proclaimed himself emperor Napoleon III. Marx describes how, beginning with the revolution of 1789, the French state bureaucracy took measures that prepared for the class rule of the bourgeoisie, only for the state, in the form of Bonaparte, to then make itself independent. Yet even though the Bonapartist regime was characterized by an autonomous executive, it nonetheless did not cease to be 'the engine of the national war of Capital against Labour'.[26] Friedrich Engels called Bonapartism – or militaristic state authoritarianism – 'the religion of the bourgeoisie'.[27] And Marx notes that under imperial domination (the reign of Napoleon III from 1853 to 1870 is referred to as the 'Second Empire'), 'bourgeois society, free of political concerns, attained a development – industrial and commercial – that it had not otherwise hoped to have done'.[28]

This could just as well have been a description of Turkey, where the capitalists have been well served by the authoritarian state. Indeed, Turkish intellectuals have drawn attention to what appear to be striking parallels between Erdoğan and Louis Bonaparte, but the parallels can be extended to Turkish right-wing leaders in general: they may come to power democratically, but they invariably turn out to be authoritarians. Bonaparte was also elected; he owed his ascendancy to the support of the peasantry – which has also been the case for the right in Turkey, as we will see later – and he then instituted his one-man rule, much as Erdoğan has done. Bonaparte, who professed to be the defender of the peasantry, but in reality served the bourgeoisie, can therefore stand as a model for the right-wing leaders who have ruled Turkey. As noted earlier, the Turkish right has pretended to stand by the people, and it has been able to mobilize wide popular support by appealing to nationalist and religious sentiments. So too did Bonaparte who, in the words of Marx, caressed the 'national egoism' of the peasantry of France. Napoleon III offered the popular classes illusions of imperial grandeur; Erdoğan has offered the popular classes of Turkey the spectacle of a neo-Ottoman revival. Bonaparte turned to the *lumpenproletariat* to intimidate the opposition; the Erdoğan regime has similarly on occasion called out gangs of thugs, drawn from the poorest sections of society, to attack the opposition.

But the socioeconomic driver of Erdoğan's and his conservative party's rise to power was a new capitalist class that had grown strong in the religiously conservative, Anatolian heartland of Turkey. The liberal left saw this class as an agent of freedom: unlike the original, 'tired' bourgeoisie of the country – which has been fostered by the state, benefiting from state tenders and from close relations with the bureaucracy in general – this new bourgeoisie was deemed to be 'authentic' and naturally inclined to be also politically liberal because it owed its ascent to its ability to compete on the global market. Its ascent was taken to herald the next step of liberalization: political freedom. It is a widely held assumption in political science that the growth of the middle class paves the way for democratization as this class demands more freedom and government accountability. But the political record of the middle classes is in fact mixed, and the Turkish case does not bear out the theory. The liberal left was nonetheless jubilant when Erdoğan's party won a landslide: 'AKP's election victory shows that a real bourgeois revolution has taken place in Turkey. Turkey's authentic bourgeoisie has finally emerged victorious from the power struggle that it has waged against the military and civilian bureaucrats during the last century', wrote one socialist intellectual.[29]

The new Turkish capitalists who were the drivers of Erdoğan's rise were baptized 'Anatolian Calvinists', and they were hailed in mainstream liberal Western media as an example of what wonders neoliberal globalization and freedom from state intervention can allegedly work. But the liberal theory suffered from two major flaws: first, it assumed that economic liberalism must necessarily stimulate political liberalism; second, it exaggerated the importance of independent entre-preneurial initiative. In fact, the new middle class of Turkey owed its rise as much to state support as it did to globalization. The new Anatolian businesses had also, as has always been the case in Turkey, benefited from the shepherding of the state. Indeed, the pattern of the Turkish political economy has never changed: the process of capital accumulation has remained intertwined with politics, with the government intervening to support privileged business interests. Yet the liberal left sees this in a different light: 'The developing bourgeoisie could never trust the bureaucracy; it believed that the state elite used its power arbitrarily.'[30] In fact, the interests of the bourgeoisie have been more than well served, even though the arbitrariness of the state may on occasion have been a nuisance for individual businessmen. The inconvenience of having to 'deal' with the state bureaucracy to secure lucrative contracts has been more than outweighed by the services the Turkish state has rendered the bourgeoisie by keeping the working class pacified.

In the 1970s, Marxist theorists clashed in a well-known debate on the question of the relationship that the state in a capitalist society entertains with capitalist interests: Ralph Miliband held that the contemporary capitalist state maintains an intimate relation with the bourgeoisie through personal bonds, educational connections and commercial ties. Nicos Poulantzas meanwhile, expanding on Marx's *Eighteenth Brumaire of Louis Bonaparte*, argued that the state's doings are relatively autonomous from class interests, at least in the short and medium term. In *Eighteenth Brumaire*, Marx portrays a state that is not a mere committee of bourgeois politicians, but an autonomous agent. However, as noted above, Marx also argued that the bourgeoisie recognized that state authoritarianism was in its own best class interests, and, as we saw, Engels mockingly called Bonapartism the 'religion of the bourgeoisie'. These concepts apply well to the Turkish case: bourgeois interests have been served by a string of Bonapartes from Atatürk to Erdoğan. Indeed, bourgeois ideology itself was introduced in Turkey by a Bonapartist state. We will now see how that happened, and how Ottoman ethnic and religious divides conjugated with capitalism to shape an authoritarian legacy that has proved to be lasting.

CHAPTER THREE

Capitalist Foundation

The Ottoman Impasse

The historian Neil Faulkner reminds us that history is driven by the interaction of three engines: the accumulation of knowledge, technique and productivity; the struggle between rival ruling classes for control of surplus; and the struggle between classes over the size and distribution of that surplus.[1] But as these engines of history always operate in specific natural and social contexts, they do not produce identical results: it was not a coincidence that capitalism arose in Europe, and not in Asia. The strength of the centralized state prevented the development of an independent urban bourgeoisie in medieval China, whereas the weakness of the feudal states of Europe allowed one to develop. The case of the Ottoman Empire is similar to China: the free development of economic and social forces was similarly blocked by the military-bureaucratic elite; as in China, economics served politics and the conditions for the development of a politically independent bourgeoisie were absent until the end of the eighteenth century. The Ottoman state had historically relied on a class of Armenian moneylenders, *amiras*, who served as the chief financiers of the empire. The *amiras* constituted an urban bourgeoisie in the capital Constantinople, but they did not qualify as an independent class; they were politically docile and by the mid nineteenth century their position as the chief financiers of the empire was overtaken by European bankers.

Marx and Engels coined the term 'Asiatic forms of production' to describe societies like China, Persia and the Ottoman Empire; their key characteristic was a lack of large private estates, which presented an obstacle to the take-off of classical capitalist development: in places where a landlord class did exist, pre-capitalist agricultural accumulation typically allowed for the emergence of a bourgeoisie that in later stages embarked on capitalist forms of accumulation. The Ottoman-Turkish case did not follow this script; it represented an 'Asian despotism'. Instead, the Turkish bourgeoisie emerged as the result of very specific historic circumstances. The first of these was the lack of a dominant landlord class, which was a defining feature of Ottoman society; this in turn was related to the second crucial circumstance that conditioned the formation of the bourgeoisie in Turkey: the independence of the Ottoman state from classes in society. The third circumstance was the destruction of the Christian bourgeoisie that emerged in the Ottoman Empire during the course of the nineteenth century.[2]

The Ottoman state had from the beginning ensured that no dominant landlord class could arise to challenge its authority. Sultan Mehmet II (1432-81) carried out a social 'revolution': he crushed the landed Turkic aristocratic families in Anatolia by expropriating their lands.[3] In this, as in many other respects, the Ottomans followed the tradition of the Byzantine Empire that they replaced. But this was a 'despotism' that at the same time benefited the peasantry. Ottoman state power, like the central authority of Byzantine power before it, rested on the mass of independent peasantry that constituted the tax base of the empire. The guiding, administrative principle of both Byzantine and Ottoman power was to secure the small surplus value that the mass of peasant households produced. As the peasantry was the state's tax base, the state had a vested interest in preventing local notables from expropriating the peasants' land. Administrative and legal procedures were continuously mobilized to protect the independent peasantry. However, in the eighteenth century, as central state power weakened and even waned, local notables in Anatolia seized the opportunity to try to accumulate land and power, and made an attempt in 1808 to impose a version of Magna Carta on the sultan. But this attempt to establish a feudal-aristocratic class and subordinate the sultan to it was defeated. From the beginning of the nineteenth century, Ottoman state authority was reasserted; power was re-centralized around a modernized, refashioned bureaucracy that thwarted nascent feudal-aristocratic ambitions.

The Anatolian notables were no match for the state because they had never succeeded in disempowering the peasantry; they had not managed to evict the peasants from their land and they had not been able to establish the big estates that would have given them clout against the state. The Ottoman bureaucracy maintained its power to act independently from a landowning class; this was also the case in Japan during the same period. But there was one major difference between the modernizing Ottoman state and the modernizing Japanese state of the Meiji restoration: while the Meiji bureaucracy encouraged the disempowerment of the peasantry, which turned them into a proletariat, the Ottoman bureaucracy continued to protect small peasant property ownership. As a result, European investors who had entertained hopes of establishing a plantation economy in the Ottoman Empire were forced to give up: there was simply no cheap labour to exploit in such plantations, as the peasantry had not been turned into a landless, unemployed proletariat. But the integration of the Ottoman Empire into the capitalist world system nevertheless proceeded unimpeded. The fact that the Ottoman state had been so successful in checking the power of the Anatolian class of notables – and thereby securing the existence of an independent peasantry – was to have disastrous effects in the context of this capitalist integration. European demand on the agricultural production of Anatolia set in motion a class reconfiguration that was ultimately to prove fatal for the Christians of Anatolia. If this production had been controlled by an indigenous, Muslim landlord class, then the integration of the Ottoman economy with European capitalism would probably not have produced the disaster that it did. We will soon see why.

With agricultural production dispersed throughout a multitude of small peasant holdings, there was a need for a class of middlemen, traders, to collect and transport what was produced to European markets. Christian traders in the Ottoman-ruled Levant – Anatolia, Lebanon, Egypt – had for centuries enjoyed a privileged position as middlemen; this longstanding tradition, together with their Christian religion, their cultural affinity in general with Europeans, and their language skills, all naturally made them the privileged partners of European traders and investors. The integration of the Ottoman economy with European capitalism propelled them into a much more powerful position as a class of *compradors*, trading agents and merchants. By the end of the nineteenth century, the Ottoman Christian *compradors* were evolving from middlemen into small industrial investors, setting up factories in cities across Anatolia. But the fact that they were predominantly Christians, mostly Greek-Orthodox, and to a lesser extent Armenians and Jews, meant that the question of class became intertwined with religion and ethnicity, which would prove to be an extremely combustible combination. In 1871, the British consul in the Black Sea port of Trebizond (now Trabzon) reported that 'in Anatolia, running into debt means falling into the hands of Armenian usurers':[4] the Muslim peasantry in Anatolia were being squeezed by compound interest rates of between 24 and 60 per cent charged by Armenian moneylenders, and as a result in many cases lost the ownership of their land.

In Europe in the nineteenth century, the processes of capitalist development and nation-building became mutually reinforcing. In the Ottoman Empire, by contrast, capitalist dynamics were divisive: they kindled and reinforced ethno-national tensions and destroyed any prospect there might have been of sustaining unity. Commerce with Europe changed the dynamics of Ottoman diversity. Across Europe, the ideas of the Enlightenment and the empowerment of the bourgeoisie converged to create a new ideal of equal citizenship. The French Revolution of 1789, with its notions of freedom, equality and brotherhood, exercised a powerful effect on the Ottoman world as well; above all, it inspired fear in the ruling circles, but it also stimulated new thinking: the idea that people were not subjects of a sultan to whom they owed allegiance because he was supposedly the terrestrial representative of divine power, but citizens with equal rights and duties, began to gain traction among liberal-minded intellectuals. But the Ottomans – Christians and Muslims alike – were ultimately incapable of transcending their ethno-religious differences. This was not because the co-existence of different creeds in itself represented an insurmountable barrier to the creation of a common Ottoman body politic; rather, it was because capitalist dynamics exacerbated these differences.

The sociologist and historian Karen Barkey points out that increasing trade with Europe, and the role of non-Muslims in European trade networks, led to growing economic disparity between groups in which undue emphasis was placed on religious and ethnic rivalries.[5] Being locked out of the profitable commerce with Europe because they were not Christians, Muslims naturally resented being at a disadvantage, and united in their identity in resentment. The new, Ottoman Christian bourgeoisie, meanwhile, followed the same path as its counterparts around Europe and consolidated a separate national identity, especially so in the case of the Ottoman Greek bourgeoisie. As Barkey observes, this was a recipe for inter-communal disaster.

Before the economic integration with Europe there had been no marked economic differences between Muslims and non-Muslims in the Ottoman Empire, but the particular way that capitalist integration worked, and the uneven results it produced, put the Ottoman Muslims at a clear disadvantage. Muslim traders were not only locked out of business with Europe. The Muslim rural, mercantile and artisan classes were destroyed when cheap European imports flooded the Ottoman market under the free trade regime that the Ottoman state had conceded to the European powers in 1838. Muslim society in Anatolia was destabilized; tens of thousands of workers and artisans lost their jobs. Muslims were either unemployed or employed at the lowest rank with the lowest salaries.

The Europeans who started projects in the empire hired cheap Muslim labour controlled by highly paid non-Muslim managers. For instance, Muslims filled 19 per cent of the lower positions in the Anatolian railroad project, while Christians, Greeks and Armenians occupied half of the middle rank and administrative positions.

It was no coincidence that the Ottoman Muslim ruling elite began to emphasize the Muslim identity of the state; this was a direct response to the rise of a Christian bourgeoisie, and it was an attempt to accommodate the disgruntled Muslim masses. There were popular calls for a return to a more stringent application of Islamic law, because the Muslim merchants and artisans understood their economic plight and articulated their response in religious terms. Barkey gives the example of a Muslim merchant in the mid eighteenth century who endured financial difficulties and advised the sultan to return to the application of religious law; Muslim merchants saw in the more stringent application of Islamic law a way out of the financial conundrum of the empire.[6] What looked like a religious conflict had social and economic origins, and we will see that this has since been a recurrent pattern: businessmen from religiously conservative, small-town Anatolia, who did not enjoy the same privileged relation with the state as culturally 'Westernized' businessmen and industrialists did, were to form the backbone of the Islamist movement that arose in Turkey in the late 1960s, while working-class frustration at economic inequality also 'naturally' came to be expressed in cultural and religious terms, as the economically privileged groups in society had a 'Western' cultural outlook.

A similar pattern of interpreting social conflict in ethno-religious terms was at work in the Balkan territories of the

Ottoman Empire, and it gave an impetus to the nationalist, secessionist movements there from the end of the eighteenth century. But in the Balkans the roles were partly reversed, since a Muslim landlord class controlled large estates, worked by Christian – and Muslim – peasants. The disgruntled Christian peasantry provided a strong base for the Slavic nationalism invented and propagated by urban intellectuals inspired by the nation-state idea that swept Europe in the wake of the French Revolution.

If the Anatolian Muslim notables had succeeded in establishing themselves as a landlord class in control of the agricultural surplus then they, rather than the Anatolian Christian *compradors*, would have become the interlocutors of European buyers. Then the absolutist Ottoman state would in time have faced only a 'normal' bourgeois challenge, without an aggravating ethno-religious dimension that called the identity of the state itself into question: as the Anatolian notables were Muslims, their empowerment as a landlord class, and their subsequent evolution into a capitalist class, would not have presented an existential threat to the Muslim state elite. As it was, the Ottoman Muslim state elite had to cope with an impossible dilemma: how was a bourgeoisie, whose rise not only challenged the hold of the absolutist state over society but its identity as a Muslim theocracy as well, going to be accommodated? How was nation-building going to succeed when the political and economic elites were demarcated from each other by religion? This was the Ottoman impasse.

In one of his articles in the *New York Daily Tribune* in 1854, Marx (a regular contributor to the American newspaper) outlined a democratic way out of that impasse: 'If you replace Sharia with a secular civil code, then you will ensure the

Westernization of the whole society of Byzantium [as Marx referred to the Ottoman society].[7] As we have already seen, the fate of the Ottoman Empire interested Marx and Engels; they hoped that it would survive – which would require it to make the transition to a nation state in the new, European sense – because the power that stood to gain from its demise was tsarist Russia, and a more powerful Russia would boost the forces of autocracy and reaction in Europe. The religious divide would be transcended with a secular law; it would enshrine the principle of equal citizenship and provide the framework of an Ottoman nation. That was what Marx's call for the Westernization of the Ottoman state meant. This, however, was something that the Ottoman ruling elite dreaded; not because it was irremediably reactionary, and opposed to progress and modernization as such, but because Westernization in this sense – a modern nation of equal citizens – would undermine its hold on power. The ruling elite did not cling to the supremacy of Islam out of religious piety so much as out of a sense of secular fear.

Histories of the Ottoman Empire during the nineteenth century conventionally portray it as being locked in a battle between progressive modernizers and Islamic reactionaries – which is taken to be the forerunner of the secularist-Islamist battles of the twentieth and twenty-first centuries. But on a more fundamental level, the real question at stake was how an absolutist state was going to cope with a new class challenge. What on the surface looks like a religiously motivated contempt for 'unbelievers' in fact spoke of the class fear of the 'state class'. The reasoning in an article by an Ottoman notable published in the French daily *Le Journal des Débats* in 1867 is suggestive in this regard: the article warned that giving the

Ottoman Christians equality would precipitate 'the end of Islam', as the Christians had a much higher level of education than the Muslims.[8] Yet the Ottomans did engage in a partial effort to Westernize: the equality of all subjects regardless of their religion was enshrined in law, at least nominally. But the circumscription of the Islamic law – which had codified the inferior position of non-Muslims – occurred as a result of the pressure exerted by the European great powers, not out of conviction, which limited the scope of real change. Westernization in the sense that Marx had used the term remained beyond the horizon of the Ottoman ruling elite.

But on 23 December 1876, Sultan Abdülhamid II, who had just ascended to the throne, was nonetheless pressed to promulgate a liberal constitution that introduced a constitutional monarchy and enshrined the equality of all citizens regardless of their creed, which represented a truly revolutionary step. On 19 March 1877 the young sultan convened an elected parliament with Muslim, Christian and Jewish members. Abdülhamid had no intention of abiding by a constitution that limited his power, but he needed to buy time: the empire faced revolt in the Balkans, and the threat from Russia loomed large. The Ottoman state was in desperate need of allies among the European great powers. Creating the impression that the autocratic empire was becoming a liberal monarchy was above all a way to secure the support of public opinion in Great Britain.

The author of the democratic constitution was Mithat Pasha (1822-84), the grand vizier. Mithat Pasha is a singular, exceptional figure in Ottoman history: he was a pious Muslim and a democratic reformist who truly believed in and worked for the equality of all citizens, and who encouraged their involvement in government. He was well ahead of his time. As province governor in the Danube region in what is now Bulgaria in the 1860s, he had taken the initiative of setting up a ruling Christian-Muslim council. He was also a social reformist: in the Danube, he founded the first agricultural credit cooperative in the empire, and later, as governor in Mesopotamia (present-day Iraq), and once again on his own initiative, he introduced land reforms that broke the power of the *aghas*, the local land barons who, unlike in Anatolia, had until then been allowed a free rein over the peasantry. When a revolt broke out in Serbia, Mithat Pasha organized a voluntary military regiment composed of Muslims and Christians, and did not hesitate to add the Christian cross to the regimental banner, alongside the Muslim crescent. In his memoirs, Mithat Pasha took pride in relating how he paraded the mixed regiment with its crescent and cross through the streets of Constantinople for everybody to behold.[9] He wanted to set an example of common, Ottoman patriotism, and he noted that the promise of a democratic constitution had indeed stimulated the patriotism of the Ottoman Christians. The latter had previously been exempt from military service; instead, they had had to pay a special tax. But a central aspect of the nineteenth-century attempts to establish the equality of all citizens, indeed of the very notion and sense of a shared Ottoman citizenship, was the conscription of Christians and Jews into the imperial armed forces. This was, however, an extremely controversial step, and the idea was met with fierce resistance within the Muslim state establishment, the Muslim population, and among Christian community leaders. However, a sense of Ottoman patriotism was emerging among the Christians, and many of them showed a readiness to serve their country in uniform.

With the promulgation of the new constitution in 1876, the empire appeared to be on the threshold of a democratic revolution. The developments in Constantinople were followed closely by democrats in Europe, and Marx and Engels were among those who felt encouraged by the prospect of a Turkish revolution. They had great expectations of Mithat Pasha, not only because he was a well-intentioned democratic reformer, but because he had a large following among the masses. Interestingly, he was not only capable of transcending the religious divide between Muslims and Christians, he was equally able to establish a following among Muslim preachers and the students at the religious seminars in the capital, who typically hailed from destitute backgrounds. This was also something that Marx and Engels found particularly promising.[10] Indeed, the emergence of a social and democratic reformer able to establish a following among the pious lower classes remains to this day the key to breaking the vicious cycle of authoritarianism in Turkey.

The sultan recognized the threat Mithat Pasha posed to him. In February 1877, before the new parliament even had been convened, Abdülhamid dismissed Mithat Pasha as grand vizier and sent him into exile in Europe. The forces of autocracy prevailed: a year later, in January 1878, the sultan suspended the constitution, dissolved the parliament, and placed its most outspokenly liberal members under arrest. A terrible fate awaited Mithat Pasha: in 1881, he was incarcerated in Taif in Hijaz, and three years later was put to death by strangulation, most likely on the orders of the sultan.

It would take nearly a century before another leader with a similar profile emerged on the political scene in Turkey: Bülent Ecevit, Turkey's social democratic leader in the 1970s, was inspired by and identified himself with Mithat Pasha. Both were democrats who defied an established, autocratic political and social order; both explored ways to decentralize power and experimented with projects for rural, local development. Ecevit revived the agricultural-industrial village development idea that Mithat Pasha had implemented as governor of the Danube. Both posed major threats to the system because they combined a zeal for social change and democratic reform with an ability to reach out to the pious masses. It is this – as we shall see – that makes Ecevit such an interesting case to study. Ecevit argued that Mithat Pasha should be seen as the forerunner of social democracy in Turkey. What is beyond doubt is that he deserves the credit for having introduced the idea of democracy and for having launched the first economic reforms in the interest of the broad mass of the people. Ecevit was spared the violent end that Mithat Pasha met, even though it was, as we will see later, a narrow escape; but he was nonetheless also imprisoned and banned from politics. Ecevit bitterly concluded that Mithat Pasha's tragic end had set a depressing pattern: 'Whoever tries to give the people a stronger say over politics and economics faces tough obstacles or grave accusations and punishments'.[11]

After the demise of Mithat Pasha, and without a parliament to worry about, the despot Abdülhamid established a repressive regime that emphasized Islam as the binding glue of the empire. In 1894 and 1895, the first large-scale massacres of Armenians took place in eastern Anatolia and in Constantinople. They earned Abdülhamid the nickname 'The Red Sultan' in Europe. Modern scholarship tends to take a more nuanced view of Abdülhamid,[12] but there is no question that he was responsible for what happened to his Christian subjects, and although there is no evidence that he personally issued orders to have Armenians killed, he manifestly refused to take action to defend them, even though some in his own government pleaded in favour of their protection. Abdülhamid justified his refusal by saying that he, the caliph, the commander of the faithful, could not reasonably order Muslim soldiers to open fire on fellow Muslim citizens to stop them from killing Christians. There was a twisted sort of political 'rationale' to this: after the secession of the Christian provinces in the Balkans, 70 per cent of the population of the empire was Muslim, and Abdülhamid made the deliberate choice to opt for an 'Islamic' exit from the Ottoman impasse, seeking to build unity and secure his power by emphasizing Muslim religious bonds.

The massacres of the Armenians represented the violent side of the coin; the other side of Abdülhamid's response to the challenge that the Christians in general and the Christian bourgeoisie in particular posed was to invest in creating a Muslim middle class to replace the well-educated Christians, and to provide the Ottoman state with an ethno-religiously reliable social base. The educational disparity between Christians and Muslims in Anatolia was in part a result of the American protestant missionary activity during the course of the nineteenth century; the missionaries had established a network of schools across Anatolia, to the benefit of Christians. To counter this, Abdülhamid made it a priority to establish public schools in the Anatolian provinces. By the time he was overthrown in 1909 by the Young Turks – a middle-class movement whose members ironically owed their social rise to the expansion of education among the Muslim population during Abdülhamid's reign – the sultan's goal of fostering a Muslim professional middle class had been a success.

The Christian bourgeoisie, however, was still in command of the economy. The *compradors* controlled trade with Europe and most of the small industry that existed was in non-Muslim hands: 80 per cent of the factories – totalling 214 in 1913 – were owned by non-Muslims. The Young Turks were determined to carry on the project of creating a Muslim Turkish middle class that Abdülhamid had begun in order to secure the power of the state: one of the leading ideologues of the new Turkish nationalism that evolved during the last decades of the empire stated that 'the foundation of the state in our era is the bourgeoisie'.[13] In the minds of the Young Turks, capitalism and the creation of a capitalist class were intertwined with the fate of the state; the survival of the state and the continued rule of their party, the CUP, depended on a 'national' capitalism.

The Young Turks launched a programme of social and political engineering to create a bourgeois base for their power and in order to bring about a Turkish nation state. As one CUP minister put it, the government had undertaken to 'create a bourgeois class like there are in the civilized countries' with the understanding that 'this class will ensure the continued existence of the Committee of Union and Progress'.[14] The statement captures the essence of the symbiotic relation between the authoritarian Turkish state and the Turkish bourgeoisie that has persisted for the last hundred years: the state has fostered the bourgeoisie, and the bourgeoisie has in return, as the CUP minister expected it would, provided the class base for authoritarian state power.

In 1913 and 1914, the Young Turk government called on the Muslim population to boycott Greek and Armenian stores. But it was the First World War that offered the opportunity to evict the Christian bourgeoisie and redistribute its wealth to a

Muslim Turkish bourgeoisie. The war finished off the Ottoman Empire, but even though the Young Turk government was defeated militarily, it was nonetheless victorious in the class war: it succeeded in destroying the Ottoman bourgeoisie. It was this class victory that cleared the way for the emergence of modern Turkey, a state with a 'national economy' and endowed with a 'national bourgeoisie'.

Armenian Booty

After the loss of the Balkans, the Ottoman government feared that the partition of Anatolia would follow. In February 1914, Russia had imposed an agreement that put the easternmost Ottoman provinces bordering Russia under international supervision, with the stated objective of ameliorating the position of the Armenians. The Armenians were indeed embattled: they suffered at the hands of the Kurdish tribes, and the Circassians who had fled from the Russian Caucasus at the end of the nineteenth century laid claim to their lands. The Ottoman authorities provided them with no protection. The Armenians did not constitute a majority in any of these provinces, but the Ottoman government feared that the reform agenda that Russia had imposed was the prelude to the creation of an Armenian state in Anatolia under Russian auspices. The Ottoman government indeed had good reason to assume that this was the case, given its recent historical experience. One of its first acts upon entering the First World War as an ally of Germany was to annul the treaty with Russia.

Revisionist Turkish historians hold that the Young Turks in fact chose to enter the war because they saw it as an opportunity to bring a 'final solution' to the Armenian question, while other historians argue that the genocide was the result of wartime conditions. Before the war broke out, the Young Turk government had launched an ethnic cleansing programme against the Ottoman Greeks to drive them out of the country, which lends credibility to the claim that the genocide was an idea that germinated before the war and may even have been a motive for entering it. However that may be, the Young Turk government believed that Armenian national aspirations posed a threat to Turkish national survival. There is no question that the Armenian question weighed heavily on the minds of the Young Turks as they deliberated over their options when Europe went to war in the summer of 1914; in secret, they even offered Russia, the Ottomans' arch-enemy, an alliance in exchange for its abandonment of the Armenian reform it was trying to impose on the Ottoman Empire. The Russian foreign minister Sergei Sazonov flatly refused the offer. The Young Turks concluded that St Petersburg was set on the dismemberment of the empire, and that their only option was to ally with Germany.

The key decisions to annihilate the Armenian community were taken in meetings during February and March 1915 between the interior minister – later grand vizier – Talat Pasha, one of the Young Turk triumvirs, and two other members of the Central Committee of the ruling party, the CUP, Doctor Bahaeddin Şakir and Doctor Mehmed Nazım.[15] There is no transcript of their meetings, but Ottoman documents and contemporary memoirs suggest that this was the case. Şakir took charge as operational chief of the special militia, which was made up of the liberated criminals who conducted the genocide together with the regular gendarmerie. The three men agreed on the necessity of dealing with 'the enemy within' because of 'the oppositional stance that the Armenians had taken toward Turkey and the assistance that they were affording to the Russian army'.[16]

In 1924, the Republic of Turkey, which had been founded the year before, accounted for less than a tenth of the non-Muslim population that had lived in the Ottoman Empire in 1908. The annihilation of the Ottoman Armenians during the First World War and the subsequent expulsion of Greek population from Anatolia resulted in the total de-Christianization of the peninsula. The annihilation and expulsion of the Christians also meant that the mostly Greek and Armenian bourgeois class had disappeared (it also included Jews, but they were never viewed as a threat by the Ottoman state). The population exchange between Turkey and Greece decided in Lausanne in 1923 exempted the Greek population of Constantinople, which had now officially been renamed Istanbul. A small part of the former Ottoman Christian bourgeoisie was thus allowed to continue its 'business as usual' – but only for the time being. During the Second World War, non-Muslim businesses were subjected to expropriating taxation that signalled there was no future for them in Turkey. In 1942, non-Muslims were subject to a property tax ten times higher than that paid by Muslims, which precipitated an exodus of non-Muslims from Istanbul after the war. The Istanbul pogrom against the Greeks in 1955 was the final straw. A history that had begun when Greek colonists founded Byzantium in 657 BC, present-day Istanbul, was over. Today, there are only a handful of Greeks left in the city.

The Ottoman Christian bankers, traders, craftsmen and small-scale industrialists who had been either killed or expelled from their homeland had left behind their capital.

During the First World War, the Ottoman government conducted a massive programme of wealth transfer. The Young Turks engaged in what might be termed business engineering: the savings of the Ottoman Christians, as well as their trading companies, craft shops, agricultural properties and industries, were expropriated by the state and handed over to selected individuals, trustworthy Muslim citizens who were going to form a new Turkish bourgeoisie. The destruction of the Ottoman Christians – with the Armenian genocide and the ethnic cleansing of the Greeks – had a marked class accent. Geostrategic and economic motives were intertwined, but the confiscation of Armenian property answered primarily to an 'existential' imperative: the dispossession of the Armenians ensured that there would be no physical bonds left between those who survived the genocide, or relatives in other parts of the world, and the land of Anatolia. A purely Turkish homeland – with a safely 'national economy' – would thus be secured. As I have noted, the Young Turks expected that a 'national bourgeoisie' would provide their authoritarian, nationalist state with a firm social footing. The confiscations that completed the genocide provided the 'dowry' for the capitalist foundation of the new state of Turkey. This was also explicitly a motive for the demographic engineering that the Young Turks carried out with such tragic success. On 6 January 1916, the Ottoman interior minister and the chief architect of the Armenian genocide, Talat Pasha, sent a telegram to all the governors in Anatolia that leaves no doubt that the confiscations were ideologically motivated, and that they were meant to serve the purpose of constructing an ethnically Turkish economy by transferring capital and goods from one ethnic group to another:

The personal property left behind by the Armenians should be conserved for long-term purposes. In order to increase the number of businesses that are owned by Muslims in our country, businesses should be set up exclusively by Muslims. The movable properties should be transferred to them under favourable conditions in order to ensure that these companies are permanently reinforced. Their founders, their managers and their representatives should be selected from among honourable citizens and among the elite. In order to allow traders and agriculturalists to benefit from the dividends, the receipts should be a half-sterling or one sterling and be registered in their names so as to avoid that the capital falls into foreign hands. The development of an entrepreneurial spirit among the Muslims needs to be encouraged. These procedures and their results will be communicated to the ministry at each stage.[17]

Talat Pasha personally supervised the annihilation of the Armenians. A former postal clerk, he knew to make the best use of the telegraph: he kept in constant communication with the provincial authorities, on a daily basis requesting details on how the displacement of the Armenians was proceeding, and filling his notebook (which has been preserved) with minute statistical information, on a provincial base, about the results of the displacement and destruction of the Armenian community. The mastermind of the genocide was just as meticulous in keeping track of the belongings of the Ottoman citizens annihilated by their own government. In June 1915, the government set up a 'Commission for Abandoned Property', in reality 33 individual sub-commissions, to take charge of and distribute 'abandoned' property. In fact, prior to being marched off to the 'final solution', the Armenians were prohibited from selling their property to foreigners or to other Christians – Greeks and Assyrians – and from transferring their property to other, non-Ottoman Armenians, or to their relatives abroad. Their bank accounts were blocked and their savings subsequently seized. Talat Pasha did not waste any time laying hands on Armenian property: already on 29 August 1915, his ministry had instructed local authorities to auction 'abandoned' property to the local Turkish population. On 1 November 1915, the interior ministry ordered the authorities in those provinces from which the Armenians had not yet been deported to draw up lists of their resident Armenian merchants, providing details about their commercial activities, their movable properties, their workshops or factories, and finally including an estimation of the added value of their entire property.[18]

The records of the 33 commissions that seized and liquidated 'abandoned' Armenian property, as well as the archival records of the Ottoman land registry office, are still guarded as state secrets by the Turkish government. Turkey has in recent years opened up many of the state archives that concern the Armenians for the use of historians, but it has doggedly refused to budge on the question of Armenian property, which is tellingly enough treated as a matter of highest national security. On 26 August 2005, the National Security Council, chaired by the president and composed of the military top brass and leading government ministers, decreed that the records should remain secret. The European Union had demanded their publication, and the government of then Prime Minister Erdoğan, which was negotiating with the EU to start membership negotiations, had had the Ottoman land registry acts and deeds scanned and translated, when the military pulled the brake. The National Security Council decreed that:

> The Ottoman archives that have been conserved at the general directory of land registry as well as land registry studies are to be kept secret and inaccessible to the public, since they are susceptible of being exploited by the defenders of the thesis that genocide took place and for making demands for restitution. ... Opening them for the use of the general public is against the interests of the state.[19]

This unscrupulous statement amounts to an official admission of Turkish guilt.

There is no question that the capitalist economy of the new state of Turkey was founded on the plunder of the Ottoman Armenians. The Turkish case stands as a perfect illustration of Marx's words that 'Capital is born covered in blood and filth'. The only thing that remains to be determined is the exact extent to which the plundering of the Armenians was indispensable for the capitalist Turkish state that came into being in 1923 and for the creation of the Turkish bourgeoisie. We will not know the answer to that until the Turkish state has released all the records. But there are ways to make estimations that give an idea of the economics of the genocide. Let us start with one example: Turkey is the world's leading producer of hazelnuts, controlling 75 per cent of global production. Before the genocide, hazelnut production was largely an Armenian business. According to Ottoman statistics from 1914, more than half of the 100 or so hazelnut producers in the empire were Armenians. During the genocide, this industry was confiscated and transferred to Muslims within the space of a few weeks. A century later, the industry produced 600,000 tons of hazelnuts yearly, and its monthly earnings stood at 624,000,000 euros.

If we turn our gaze from the mountainous Black Sea coast of Anatolia, where the hazelnut grows, to the corner of the Mediterranean coast of the peninsula that joins Syria, we face another region where looting fuelled the capitalist development of modern Turkey: former Cilicia, presently Çukurova. Here, cotton plains stretch north from the Mediterranean all the way to the massive Taurus mountain range. This is an exceptionally fertile land, agriculturally among the most productive areas of the world, and it is an engine of the Turkish economy. In 2011, Turkey was the seventh largest cotton producer in the world. The land of Cilicia – including most of its cotton estates, as well as its textile and cotton gin factories – was genocide booty as well. Cilicia was a sort of 'second Armenia', distinct from the historical Armenia which stretched from eastern Anatolia into the Caucasus, but it became home to an Armenian kingdom that against all odds managed to survive, squeezed between the Arab and Turkic expansions, and the onslaught of the Mongols, for three centuries from 1080 to 1375. Astonishingly, autonomous Armenian principalities, *melikats*, survived in the Taurus mountain range until the beginning of the twentieth century.[20]

Swamps used to cover Cilicia, until the area was drained in the early nineteenth century and the wetlands were transformed into cotton fields. With the global cotton boom in the 1860s, when the American Civil War created a demand for alternative suppliers of cotton, the producers in Cilicia got a head-start. In the mid nineteenth century, Cilician Armenian traders were well-placed to seize the opportunity that cotton offered. Armenian traders, but also Muslim tribal chiefs in the region, established big estates. Cilicia was the exception from the pattern of landowning in the rest of Anatolia: here it was not a small, independent peasantry that prevailed, but a class of big landowners, and by the mid twentieth century more than 12 per cent of the peasants had been dispossessed of their land. Çukurova is unique: nowhere else in Turkey has there been such a concentration of agricultural surplus enabling primitive capital accumulation, and nowhere else has the agricultural surplus provided such opportunities for the development of commerce and industry. Cotton production had already given an impetus for industrialization during the closing decades of the Ottoman Empire. With its textile and cotton gin industries, Cilicia was a bridgehead for capitalist industrial production in the empire. The dispossessed peasants were exploited as labourers on the cotton fields by the landlord class. The class struggles in Çukurova have provided the material for great literature: an international audience has made the acquaintance of 'Memed the Hawk', the peasant rebel who stands up to the rule of the *aghas*, the feudal landlords, as the hero of one the finest novels in Turkish literature, *Memed My Hawk*, the masterpiece by the socialist Kurdish writer Yaşar Kemal (1923-2015).

Adana, the main province of Cilicia, produced 135,000 cotton balls in 1914. In 1921, production had dropped to a mere 15,000 balls. The fields were left untended, the textile and cotton gin factories stood still. Their owners, the Armenians, had been either killed or deported from their homeland. The new owners were yet to develop the necessary skills. But by the 1950s, the population of Adana had doubled, and it used to be said that there were more Cadillacs per capita in Adana than in any city in the United States. The Ottoman interior minister, Talat Pasha, had in his usual meticulous style listed the booty in Adana: 696 buildings had been confiscated, including churches, schools, houses, farms, warehouses and factories. In 1923, the new strongman of Turkey, the heir of the Young Turks, Mustafa Kemal, honoured Adana with his presence, and in a speech to the local association of craftsmen assured them that 'The Armenians don't have the least right to this fertile land. The land belongs to you, the Turks. This country is historically Turkish; it is thus going to remain Turkish for eternity. These fertile lands are the profound and fundamental essence of Turkey.'[21] The materialistic dimension of the new Turkish nationalism could not have been better expressed. To his credit, and unlike other nationalists then and now, Kemal at least did not attempt to mystify the nation; he tacitly recognized that the 'essence of Turkey' was not 'spiritual' but prosaically material: rooted in the fertile land that was stolen from its owners.

Perry Anderson argues that 'Kemal was one of history's most striking examples of moral luck.'[22] Anderson points out that by accident of military appointment Kemal had been spared involvement in the Armenian genocide, and that there is a difference between taking part in a crime and gaining from one. Yet the question is whether the founder of a state based on the killing fields of genocide can be morally exempt from complicity in the foundational crime. We saw above that the Nazis approvingly recognized that Kemal's endeavour, the building of a Turkish nation state, could succeed only because the Armenians had been annihilated and the Greeks expelled. It is symbolic that all Turkish presidents – until Erdoğan – have resided in a palace that was built on booty from the genocide. When Kemal took up residence in Angora (present-day Ankara) the local authorities offered him a mansion on the hill of Çankaya that was later expanded into a palatial compound. Few Turks know that the mansion was stolen: it belonged to the Armenian Kasapyans, a rich bourgeois family that in 1915 had been ordered to leave Angora. They had to abandon their lucrative goat wool business, but at least the Kasapyans survived the deportation since one of the family members, employed by a foreign company that operated railroads in the empire, was able to organize their transfer to the relative safety of Constantinople. Prominent members of the Armenian community in the capital had been arrested on 24 April 1915, and had subsequently been dispatched to Anatolia where they perished or were killed, but otherwise the Armenian population of Constantinople was spared the fate of the Anatolian Armenians.

Kemal hardly harboured any moral reservations about moving into the stolen mansion, especially not since his own mother and sister had had to leave behind their home, his childhood home in Saloniki, and become refugees when that city was lost to the Ottomans in 1912 during the First Balkan War. In the unlikely event that Kemal gave the owners of the house into which he moved any thought, he would not have found their fate to be any worse than that of his own family. This is indeed a common stance among Turks: the genocide of the Armenians is not really denied, but simply shrugged off; most Turks equate the ethnic cleansing of the Muslims in the Balkans during the last decades of the Ottoman Empire with the anni-hilation of the Christians in Anatolia. In their eyes, the former ultimately justified the latter. The pattern that was established with Kemal – the building of the Turkish presidency on stolen property – has been perpetuated with Erdoğan. When he became president in 2014, Erdoğan moved into a 1,000-room presidential complex that is bigger than both the Versailles Palace and the Kremlin, and which was illegally constructed in a forest reserve bequeathed to the nation by Atatürk. Erdoğan thus also appropriated property illegally. A court ruled that the building of the presidential complex on the site was illegal, but its ruling was dismissed by the government. It was a symbolic act when what Kemal had bequeathed, the forest reserve, was illegally cut down to make room for a new presidential palace, just as the first Turkish presidential palace had been built on stolen property. Disregard for legality marked the beginnings of both the Turkish state and Turkish capitalism, and that is a pattern that has persisted.

Rich Cilicia was a ravaged land after the genocide, but it was here that one of the giants of Turkish capitalism, the Sabancı business empire, was born. Enter Hacı Ömer,[23] the archetypal Turkish industrial capitalist entrepreneur. Ömer was a boy of 14 when he arrived in the region in 1921. He had left his native village in the central Anatolian province of Kayseri, ancient Caesarea, and walked by foot nearly 500 kilometres south to find fortune in Çukurova, where the 'abandoned' cotton fields and textile factories beckoned. He was to be richly rewarded. However, Ömer was not alone in making the trek from Kayseri to Adana. His native province counted many Muslim merchants who hurried to take possession of the real estate, commerce and industry that was on offer in Çukurova after the annihilation and exodus of the Armenians. In many cases, these new capitalists of the new state of Turkey benefited from the good connections they enjoyed with the authorities. Young Ömer could barely read and write, he was an orphan, and obviously did not enjoy close relations with the state offi-cialdom, but he was helped by his family connections with the established merchants of his native Kayseri who put him in touch with the right people in the bureaucracy. Hacı Ömer was an extremely fortunate beneficiary of the redistribution of 'abandoned' property; with this as a foundation, he built the second largest industrial and commercial conglomerate in Turkey. We will later see his son, Sakıp Sabancı, endorse Erdoğan. Hacı Ömer Sabancı Holding employs nearly 60,000 workers, is active in 16 countries, and its activities range from financial services and energy to cement, retail and industrials. The holding has entered into partnerships with such inter-national business giants as Mitsubishi, Bridgestone, Philip Morris and Carrefour.

On the face of it, Hacı Ömer fits the bill of a 'self-made man' perfectly: here is a poor peasant boy who sets off in life with two empty hands. But a closer look reveals that, like most other early Turkish entrepreneurs, it was access to looted property that gave him a head-start. For those who were morally unscru-pulous, Çukurova was a promised land. Barely a decade after his arrival in Çukurova, Hacı Ömer shared the ownership of a cotton gin factory, he had acquired two olive oil factories and the first of four farms, of 1,000 hectares. He admitted that the state had handed him the cotton fields. His business associate had played a leading role in the massacres of the Armenians that took place in Adana in 1909. The Sabancı family has not forgotten what it owes to Adana. They have financed schools, libraries, cultural centres and Adana's grand mosque, which is for now Turkey's biggest (the grand mosque that Erdoğan is having built in Istanbul is going to beat it when it is completed). But for some family members there is perhaps also a sense of guilt or moral remorse nagging somewhere deep down: the university in Istanbul that the Sabancıs own distinguished itself by being open to research into the Armenian genocide, and it has hosted a conference on the massacres in Adana in 1909, when at least 20,000 Armenians were killed by a Muslim mob. That is maybe not a coincidence.

Hacı Ömer was exceptionally successful, but he was by no means unique. The background to the Sabancı success story is a perfect illustration of the genesis of the Turkish bourgeoisie. As the French journalists Laure Marchand and Guillaume Perrier note, in their excellent book about how the Armenian genocide continues to haunt Turkish society: 'The entrepreneurs have blood on their hands, others have "only" shamelessly profited from the opportunities that the crime presented them with. And they enjoyed the benediction and the assistance of the state.'[24] In his novel *The Birds Have Also Gone*, Yaşar Kemal – who, as noted above, was a native of Çukurova, and who had worked on the cotton fields as a boy – tells the story of a Kurdish family that has to flee to Adana during the First World War. The displacement of populations in Anatolia during and after the First World War is the topic of several of Kemal's novels. In *The Birds Have Also Gone* he has the mother of the character İsmail Ağa instruct her son upon his departure to under no condition accept either a house or a field that had belonged to the Armenians when he arrives in Çukurova, because, she says, when a nest has been abandoned by its owner, another bird will not find peace of mind there: 'He who has destroyed a nest cannot make it his own. When you sow unhappiness, you will only reap unhappiness.'[25] Yaşar Kemal wrote these lines in the late 1970s, when the violence of the far right was claiming thousands of victims among leftist intellectuals, students, trade union activists and Alevis. It is not implausible that those unhappy times inspired Kemal to write about how 1915 was going to mark Turkey's future. There is certainly a historical continuity at work: born covered in blood and filth, Turkish capitalism has continued to sow unhappiness in society. In the 1970s, the obstacle that needed to be cleared was the left. There is no reason to think that looting the 'nests' of the Armenians caused the Hacı Ömers of the Turkish bourgeoisie any particular chagrin; the business barons enjoyed pleasant lives and bourgeois comforts. But did the circumstances of its genesis nonetheless mar the Turkish bourgeoisie? Is this the reason why it has not challenged the authoritarianism of the state? That is certainly the view of thinkers on the liberal left.

The leading liberal leftist Ahmet İnsel, who, as we saw in the preceding chapter, argues that the Turkish bourgeoisie has not been able to develop into a political force of its own, locates the source of this supposed political timidity and the origin of the bourgeois embrace of the authoritarian state in the plunder of the properties and capital of the Ottoman Christians. He argues that their complicity in the crime weaved lasting bonds of solidarity with the state.[26] This is a common line of reasoning among Turkish liberal leftists and liberal intellectuals; they hold that the bourgeoisie is by its nature an agent of democracy, and that it is only the Turkish bourgeoisie's 'debt' to the state that has prevented it from accomplishing what is held to be its normal historical role. This is nonsensical. The bourgeoisie cannot be whitewashed; its class interests have fuelled violence. Just as the drive to create a 'national capitalism' was one, if not the only, driving force behind the annihilation of the Ottoman Armenians, so, as we will later see in detail, was the fascist campaign of violence against the left and a murderous military dictatorship instrumental in establishing the neoliberal order in Turkey.

Middle-class Radicalism

During the first decades of the Turkish republic, however, in the 1920s and 1930s, the ideology of the bourgeoisie was distinctly progressive; at this early stage of capitalist development, it was bourgeois radicalism that answered to the needs of the moment. But it was an ephemeral moment. The onset of the Cold War at the end of the 1940s introduced a new ideological dynamic, and bourgeois radicalism was duly abandoned and replaced with bourgeois conservatism as the ideology of the ruling class of Turkey. We will see in the next chapter how, starting in the 1940s, the influence of religion was restored by the ruling bourgeois parties. What was then established would prove to be a winning formula for the right: pro-business liberalism in combination with religious conservatism for mass consumption. The middle-class radicalism that the Kemalist revolution bequeathed has survived as the lifestyle of the secular bourgeoisie, but class interests have led bourgeois politicians to embrace religious conservatism as a political tool. This contradiction between culture and class has trapped the secular bourgeoisie of Turkey in an existential impasse: its cultural preferences clash with its class interests; to defend its material privileges, the bourgeoisie has had to make cultural concessions to Islamic conservatism.

We saw above that the Marxist historian Perry Anderson has described the transformation of Turkey in the 1920s and 1930s as a strange one, a cultural revolution without a social revolution. But in fact the Kemalist revolution cleared away the remnants of a theocratic order that stood in the way of capitalism. Anderson notes that 'there was no anti-capitalist impulse in Kemalism'.[27] On the contrary, the impulse was pro-capitalist. Following upon the genocide that had secured start-up capital, the Kemalist reforms provided the capitalist foundation with its legal framework, removing many of the obstacles that had prevented the establishment and development of the capitalist mode of production. The secularization of the legal system had begun already during the last century of the Ottoman Empire, but the Islamic sharia law, which had hardly changed in a millennium, still undergirded most areas. The application of secular law in commerce, contract law, property, legacy and family law laid the foundations for a modern, bourgeois society. The Turkish civil code of 1926 was imported wholesale from Switzerland. Lacking any reference whatsoever to Islam, Turkey's family law is unique among Muslim countries. What mattered crucially for the development of a capitalist economy was that private property rights were finally given full legal recognition. The first step in this direction had been taken with the land law in 1858, when private property rights had been accorded a limited recognition, and when the possibility of officializing private ownership of land had been opened. But what about all the other cultural reforms: the ban on religious schools, the expansion of secular education, the rules on men's headgear, the adoption of the Latin alphabet and the Western calendar, making Sunday the weekly holiday instead of Friday, the recognition of gender equality, at least on paper? What did they have to do with helping capitalist development along? In fact, these changes also conformed to the logic of an emerging, bourgeois society and to the needs of a nascent bourgeoisie that wanted to be released from ancient customs and religious and social tradition.

The Kemalist revolution is usually, and with good reason, compared to the French Revolution, which similarly took on religion and tradition, propelled the bourgeoisie to the forefront of society, and represented the passage from a feudal order to capitalism. But as Anderson remarks, the scale and speed of the Kemalist assault on religious tradition and household custom, embracing faith, time, dress, family and language, remain unique in the so-called Muslim world.[28] In no other Muslim country has the development of bourgeois society and a capitalist economy been accompanied by such all-encompassing change and break with religious tradition. This begs for an explanation. What was it that made Turkey unique in this respect? Does it boil down to Atatürk's eccentricity, as when he decided that state radio was not going to broadcast Turkish music, but only classical Western music, or when he ruled that the president and the speaker of the parliament should be dressed up in a tail coat as if they were attending a ball? Every president until Erdoğan complied with that odd custom. More seriously, people who came to Ankara from the countryside in the 1930s were not permitted to enter the city centre in 'non-European' clothes. The tail coat, the Panama hats that Atatürk fancied wearing, and the Latin characters were all evidently meant to signal that the new Turkish nation was a Western nation; but what is overlooked is that they also expressed the class interests of a rising bourgeoisie. This singular operation of cultural conversion can in fact only be understood against the background of a particular, formative historical experience. The Kemalist reformers had come of age in a late Ottoman society where the non-Muslim bourgeoisie enjoyed a privileged position; they were embittered Young Turks who had seen how non-Muslim businessmen, the *compradors*, the bankers, entrepreneurs and craftsmen had all prospered. They knew that the Ottoman Christian's business success and prosperity had everything to do with their culture and religion, which had made them the privileged interlocutors of fellow-Christian European investors and merchants. Being Muslim meant being cut out of lucrative business. It was against this background that Turkey's bourgeois revolutionaries came to the radical conclusion that they had to show that they were not Muslims. The reforms that broke with the Muslim religion and culture conveyed a message to the West: deep down, they amounted to a plea not to think of the Turks as Muslims, and to give them access to capital.

During the late Ottoman era, class divisions had been ethnically and religiously coloured; in a similar fashion, class, cultural and religious identities also became intertwined in the new state of Turkey. The twin processes of capitalist foundation and culture revolution produced a new bourgeoisie of capitalists and professionals, civil servants, lawyers and intellectuals, that adopted the new Western mores, and which was cut off from the broad masses of the population. For the peasant population of Anatolia, as well as for the working class and the poor in the cities, these modern mores and the permissive lifestyle imported from Europe – it was especially sensitive that women stepped out in public unveiled – were not only a provocative break with religious tradition and household custom, they were also resented because they were identified with the ruling class, the rich and the educated. The pattern from the late Ottoman era has thus persisted: class resentment and cultural alienation have gone hand in hand, and the conflation of class and culture has benefited the right. We will see in the next chapter how the right pulled off the feat of securing the rule of the privileged few by posing as the defender of the culture and religion of the broad masses. But this bourgeois conservatism has ultimately been allowed to prevail because the enlightenment pretentions of middle-class radicalism have dug a deep trench between the left and the working class. Middle-class radicalism has, as noted earlier, defined the Turkish left and confined it to fighting for enlightenment against reaction. However, being guided by the belief that everything belonging to the past merits nothing but pity and contempt has been self-defeating for the left. The words of Jules Guesde, a leading French socialist journalist and politician, who reproached the left in France in the aftermath of the defeat of the Paris commune in 1871 for neglecting 'the real and unique enemy: capitalism, for the sake of an imaginary adversary: clericalism',[29] apply very well to the left in Turkey. This is not to say that religious reaction has been an imaginary adversary, and the struggle against reaction illegitimate, but rather that the progressive aspirations of middle-class radicalism have bred prejudices against the culture of the broad masses. Turkish progressives have seen religious reaction in everything that belongs to popular, religious culture, and that has played into the hands of the populist right. In Turkey, middle-class radicalism was frozen in time: the progressive tradition has continued to nurse the legacy of the culture revolution of the 1920s and 1930s, which has kept the popular masses alienated from the left, except when, as we will see, the social democratic leader Ecevit set out to correct what he called the 'historical mistake' of Kemalism, the belief that religion was synonymous with reaction. But before that we will look at how the right won over the people in the first place.

CHAPTER FOUR

How the Right Won the People

'Tribunes of the People'

On 14 May 1950, the first free election was held in Turkey. The election ended the one-party rule that had lasted since the foundation of the republic in 1923. The Republican People's Party (CHP), founded by Atatürk, was crushingly defeated by the opposition Democrat Party (DP), which had been founded only four years earlier. This was a liberal-conservative party that combined commitment to the market and an appeal to tradition in equal measure. Perry Anderson remarks that 'The recipe for its rule was a paradox rare in the Third World, a liberal populism.'[1] The Democrats' election slogan was 'It's enough! It's now up to the people to decide!' It is a slogan that has continued to resonate with the Turkish masses ever since.

The 1950 election established the synonymy of the right and the people; the right appropriated the cause of the people, and populism has since remained a staple of conservative rhetoric, whether secular or Islamic. The DP received over 55 per cent of the votes. It was to govern for a decade – winning with over 58 per cent of the votes in 1954, slipping to 48 per cent but still winning in 1957, the last election that it could contest – until it was ousted in a military coup almost ten years to the day

Figure 2 The conservative prime minister Adnan Menderes in rural Anatolia. Since the historic election in 1950, which the right won by a landslide, the masses in Anatolia have most of the time flocked to the populist right.

after its historic victory, on 27 May 1960. The DP's historic landslide holds radically different meanings for Turkey's right and left. While the right celebrates it, the left deplores it. For the right, 1950 is a shining moment, the 'victory of the people'. For the left, 1950 was the moment when 'religious reaction' prevailed.

In the words of Süleyman Demirel, the leading right-wing politician from the 1960s to the 1990s, 14 May 1950 was 'a truly great victory for the Turkish people': 'For the first time since a state came into being in this country nine hundred years ago, power had changed hands peacefully, without bloodshed, at the ballot box by the expression of the sovereign will of the people.'[2] The liberals and the liberal left have joined the right in interpreting and hailing 1950 as a 'people's revolution' against the bureaucratic oligarchy. But for the Turkish left otherwise, 1950 was a 'counter-revolution' that restored the role of religion in society; socialists tend to join the dominant Kemalist left in deploring the victory of the Democrat Party. Yet both interpretations are equally superficial and beside the point. Neither accounts for the true context of the liberal-conservatives' rise to power, the political coming of age of the new bourgeoisie that the state had fostered. By the mid 1940s, this class was ready to fly on its own. However, it could not emancipate itself from the bureaucracy and assume the leadership of the state without aligning with the peasant masses. Their role was crucial, but they were nonetheless a subsidiary to the dominant class. The 1950 election was not the victory of the 'people' or of 'religious reaction', but that of a commercial and landowning bourgeois class that mobilized both to ascend to political power. And this in turn established a pattern that has endured: although they have served the interests of the affluent classes, the parties of the right have maintained the support of the small peasantry, the lower middle class and the working class, and have kept being re-elected with vast majorities since the 1950s, except when they were challenged by a social democracy that knew to give voice to the concerns of the masses. The Turkish right has addressed both the material and the non-material aspirations of the masses by manufacturing a political antagonism between the silent Muslim majority and a Westernizing minority. By assuming the role of tribune of the poor and powerless, defender of the culture, faith and integrity of the labouring masses, the right has defused class politics and maintained itself in power. It has channelled the

Figure 3 Hat off for the people: the conservative leader Süleyman Demirel assured the people that 'for us, you are the highest being there is'.

frustration of the lower classes toward the bureaucracy, away from the economic interests that the bureaucrats in fact serve.

'The elite and the bureaucrats have trouble liking and accepting the people and its representatives.'[3] These words belong to Demirel, but all of the leaders the right – from his predecessor Adnan Menderes, the leader of the Democrat Party, to Erdoğan – have appealed to the masses with the same message: that they were on their side against the state elite. The rhetoric of the right has exalted the people, held to be culturally pure and morally noble. Demirel assured them that 'We do not get angry with you, we do not call you ungrateful, we do not get cross at you, because for us you are the greatest being there is.'[4] The people could count on the right to stand up to the elite, the urban snobs: 'we will not waver in standing up against those who call you backward, reactionary, ignorant or whatever, we will be there for you if they insult you by calling you lazy', Demirel typically pledged in an election speech in the 1960s. Demirel was a country boy from a small village in western Anatolia, and his populism had an aura of authenticity. Party propaganda made good use of his peasant credentials, presenting him as *Çoban Sülü*, Shepherd Sülü, in reference to the duties the conservative leader had once performed during his childhood. For the masses, Demirel was 'one of us', no matter the fact that he had long since joined the social elite and looked after the interests of big business rather than those of the poor and powerless. The populist illusion worked its magic for Demirel, except when he was challenged by a leftist who established a rapport with the masses; ironically, the leftist in question, Bülent Ecevit, hailed not from a poor peasant background like Demirel, but from the social elite. As we will see, Ecevit made the reverse journey, from the elite to the people, in the style of many other radical politicians in other countries.

After the 1950 election the Democrat Party embraced economic liberalism, but not, as it turned out, political liberalism, and in power it became increasingly authoritarian. As we have seen, this has been a recurrent pattern. Erdoğan's Justice and Development Party is the latest example of what Perry Anderson calls 'liberal populism', which combines commitment to the market and an appeal to tradition, but which does not deliver any democratization. The 1950 victory of the DP was not the democratic turning point that the Turkish right has self-servingly made it into. But the charge of the left that 1950 was a religiously conservative 'counter-revolution' has played into the hands of the right, by sustaining the notion that the DP's rise to power represented a setback for a secularist, 'revolutionary' state bureaucracy. Erdoğan is the latest right-wing leader to have exploited the myth of 1950, posing as the heir to people's revolution, and claiming to have brought 1950 to fruition by establishing the supremacy of the people over the bureaucracy. In fact, the liberal-conservative party's victory in 1950 represented the fulfilment of the ambitions that had guided the rulers of the state since its founding. The Turkish republic had, as we have seen, nursed a capitalist economy and a bourgeoisie, a capitalist class, and the success of this endeavour was inevitably going to have political ramifications. But the left – the Kemalist left and the socialist left that has appropriated much of the ideological baggage of Kemalism – overlooks the continuity between the Kemalist and liberal-conservative populist eras when it interprets 1950 as a counter-revolution. It ignores that both the secularist reforms under Atatürk, and the restoration of the influence of religion that the DP is identified with, served the same bourgeois class interests.

As we have seen, in the 1920s and 1930s, it was bourgeois radicalism that was functional in terms of the development of a capitalist economy and society, but by the mid 1940s, an ideological adjustment imposed itself. The Turkish regime was haunted by the spectre of the threat of communism after the Second World War and the onset of the Cold War. Although Turkey had stayed out of the war, it was no secret that the regime had hoped for a Nazi victory over the Soviet Union, the heir to Turkey's historical enemy Russia. Now, the regime feared leftist subversion, which led it to embrace religion as an antidote to the temptation of socialism. After the Democrat Party came to power, the conservative restoration that was already well under way picked up pace: new mosques were built, religious schools multiplied, the call to prayer could be heard in Arabic again, and the religious fraternities began their journey from the underground to which the Kemalist regime had confined them back to the pinnacles of state power, where they soon became entrenched.

Despite appearances, 1950 was not a regime change, but a change of guard within the regime and a change of ideological accent: bourgeois radicalism yielded to bourgeois conservatism. The DP was born out of the CHP: the new president, Celal Bayar, was a former CUP activist who had played a leading role in the Anatolian civil war between Muslims and Christians after the First World War, when he administered the ethnic cleansing of the Greeks in his native region of Bursa in western Anatolia. He became a close confidant of Atatürk, who entrusted him with the task of founding and leading a state-owned bank, İş Bankası (Work Bank), which was to encourage industry. Bayar was also Atatürk's last prime minister. The leader of the DP and the new prime minister was Adnan Menderes, a rich landowner from south-western Anatolia, the location of the river that the ancient Greeks called Meander and which in Turkish has been distorted into 'Menderes'. Adnan Menderes represented the generation that came after the generation that founded the state, and he had not enjoyed a personal relation with Atatürk, although the former president had identified him as a promise for the future. It was not coincidental that the DP was headed by a former state banker and a big landowner: the founding of the party was an expression of the joint interests of the merchant and landlord factions of the bourgeoisie. But urban and rural interests were to diverge during the DP's years in power, contributing to the political crisis that precipitated the overthrow of the Menderes government in the military coup of 1960.

Business profits had soared during wartime, and the business community started to demonstrate a newfound political assertiveness against the bureaucrats. But in the countryside the wartime years had brought only more poverty, and discontent was widespread. The peasantry reeled under heavy taxation and high prices. The regime needed to be pro-active in shoring up its power, which was being undermined by the combination of bourgeois assertiveness and peasant discontent. It sought to appease the peasantry, and with this in mind decided to redistribute land. The agrarian bill introduced in 1945 by President İsmet İnönü, Atatürk's successor, did not envisage any major social revolution, nor was there any call for it among the small peasantry; as we have seen earlier, the Anatolian peasantry had historically owned its own land. The land reform bill did envisage some land redistribution from big landowners to the small peasantry, but in most cases, it simply recognized the peasants' right to ownership of state-owned land that they already cultivated. Yet that was enough to provoke a revolt of the landlords and a split in the ruling CHP, which was a coalition of big landowners like Menderes and the bureaucrats. Menderes denounced the land reform bill in speeches in parliament; Bayar, Menderes and other leading CHP dignitaries signed an open letter calling for the bill to be rescinded. In 1946 the landlord faction of the party broke ranks and formed the DP. But despite its origin in the opposition to land reform, the DP became the party of the peasants, as any party contesting elections in a country where the small peasantry constituted the vast majority inevitably had to be. That was also what had prompted the CHP to launch the land reform bill, but it came too late to save a party that was so detested, and neither did it go far enough. During the CHP's last years in power, from 1946 to 1950, 33,000 peasant households benefited from land redistribution; by contrast, during the DP's time in government, from 1950 to 1960, state-owned land was distributed to over 300,000 households.

The twofold message of the bourgeois opposition – to free the economy and religion from state intervention – had wide popular appeal. A broad coalition rallied behind the bourgeoisie. Even the banned Communist Party of Turkey actively endorsed the DP, because the new party had intimated that workers would be given the right to strike. Once in power though, the party adopted a hostile stance toward labour. The peasantry that formed the base of the DP was alienated from the Kemalist regime, not to say outright hostile to it, not only because of its interference with its customs and traditions, but because it also held the state responsible for its economic distress. Meanwhile, Menderes' free market message held out the promise of future prosperity for small producers, rather than just for profiteering merchants, as had been the case during the CHP's one-party rule. Ever since the historic 1950 election, combining religion and the market has proved to be a superior electoral strategy.

The Clash of Liberal Populism and Capitalism

By the end of the 1950s Turkey was in political turmoil. The conservative government still enjoyed broad support in the countryside, but increasingly the urban population started to turn against it. Menderes responded with repressive measures that only deepened the crisis. Critical journalists were jailed, and newspapers were shut down. Police clamped down on protesting university students. The opposition was prevented from organizing rallies. İsmet İnönü, the former president, and other CHP politicians were attacked by pro-government thugs. The conservative party was becoming desperate as the tide turned against it: even though the DP had secured another election victory in 1957, it had lost significant ground to the opposition. The party responded by setting up an investigative committee in parliament that was charged with bringing criminal charges against members of the opposition. It was clear that Menderes, who had come to power promising freedom, had turned into an autocrat and was now bent on trying to establish a full-blown, authoritarian regime.

But Menderes was out of tune with the new societal dynamics, and his authoritarian ambitions were ultimately untenable. He faced the opposition of an urban coalition that comprised industrialists, intellectuals, state functionaries, students and workers. He was in trouble because the class coalition of urban and rural bourgeois interests that had sustained his party's rise to power had split after only a few years. During the second half of the 1950s, the industrial faction of the Turkish bourgeoisie grew increasingly disgruntled with the agrarian economic populism of the DP.[5] The DP's economic policies privileged agricultural interests at the expense of the private industrial sector: while agriculture was supported with credit and tax breaks, industry was submitted to price controls and suffered from limits on credit. The conservative government also resisted the calls from business circles for national planning policies to aid industrial growth. What gave the DP its electoral advantage – the support of the peasantry – had become a trap: to retain its electoral edge, the party persisted with an agrarian economic populism that put it at odds with the interests of an assertive industrial class and with the increasingly vocal urban groups in society.

In 1946, the ruling CHP's land reform bill had, as we saw, provoked the split in the party when the big landlords, aligned with the commercial urban bourgeoisie, rebelled against the bureaucracy; a decade later, the agrarian policies of the DP similarly precipitated a party split. This time, it was the urban bourgeoisie that took issue with the landlord interests that had come to dictate government policy. It called for a redistribution of state resources from agriculture to industry. Liberal populism was at an impasse because it had not synchronized with the evolving dynamics of capitalism in Turkey. But psychology and personality also contributed to the escalation of the crisis and to its tragic conclusion. Menderes was an emotional and impulsive, not to say unbalanced, man who seems to have come to believe that he enjoyed divine protection, especially after he survived a plane crash outside London in which several of his party colleagues died. Fundamentally, he was shaped by his experience as a landlord: from an early age he had been used to being obeyed by the peasants who worked his land. His obstinate refusal to make the necessary political adjustments and his belief that he would ultimately prevail, no matter how much opposition his policies provoked, also spoke of a troubled personality and of a lack of a sense of reality. Menderes firmly believed that he embodied the popular will and that his electoral majority gave him a free hand to suspend liberties that were deemed to threaten 'order'. It has been the same story ever since: all of Menderes' successors, the leaders of the Turkish right, have held that the popular majorities they secured gave them a licence to trample on democratic and civil liberties. Erdoğan echoed the words of his idol Menderes when, during the Gezi protests in 2013, he said that democracy is the ballot box, period; democracy did not include the right to object to the decisions of the government. In almost the same words, Menderes claimed that freedom was not a licence to oppose the government, and he blamed the political violence against the opposition on the opposition itself. He argued that the only reason for the political violence that had come to plague Turkey by the end of the 1950s was the fact that the representatives of the opposition lacked good judgement, making 'unnecessary' trips across the country to hold rallies that raised political tensions. 'What's the reason for these travels?' he asked incredulously. He had at best a very limited understanding of democracy.

Yet because he was ultimately overthrown in a coup, and executed, the authoritarian-populist conservative Menderes became a 'martyr of democracy' for the right. His tragic fate has been used to maintain a long-lived and politically extremely effective myth according to which conservatives are martyrs, the victims of the state and the military, which oppresses civil society and which has not respected the popular will, until its power was crushed by Erdoğan. This is a narrative that conveniently obscures the authoritarian bent of the right-wing parties, and the fact that their own and the military's objectives have converged. It also obfuscates the fact that, far from being the underdog, the right has ruled the country, serving the interests of the business elite. Turkish politics makes no sense unless this underlying class aspect is taken into consideration. But how then do we account for the overthrow of the conservative Menderes, who came to power precisely as the representative of bourgeois interests? The answer lies in the paradox of Turkish politics: the dynamics of capitalist development have ensured that the right is dominant, but they have also made it unstable. Even though it represents dominant class interests, and has dominated the political life, the right has nonetheless often been destabilized by internal contradictions. Turkey's political course since the 1950s has partly been shaped by intra-class conflict within the ruling bourgeoisie. The underlying reality of the unbroken dominance of the interests of capitalists and their political agents is easily overlooked as the Turkish right has been weakened by the intra-bourgeois rivalries that capitalist development has kept engendering. The right's hold on power has often seemed to be tenuous at best, and conservatives have appeared to be victims of an intrusive state bureaucracy, and of the interventions of the military; this, however, is a misunderstanding, indeed a myth, but Turkish liberal leftist intellectuals have built it into the grand theory that I described in Chapter 2. This theory postulates that the defining dynamics of Turkish politics was a conflict between civil society – represented by supposedly disempowered conservatives – and the oppressive 'secularist' state elite, until civil society, the 'periphery', prevailed over the 'centre' when Erdoğan came to power. In fact, it is the civilian right's inability to negotiate the intra-class rivalries that the dynamics of capitalism has continued to produce that has on occasion hampered its exercise of power, and not any structural antagonism between it and the military or the bureaucracy. It is this inability that has provided the context for some of the turning points in modern Turkish history, from the country's first military coup in 1960 to the rise of the Islamist movement. We will see later how the rivalry between two bourgeois factions precipitated the split of the right and the founding of Turkey's first Islamist party in 1970, and how in 1997 this intra-class rivalry brought down the country's first Islamist prime minister. And we will see that the intra-bour-

geois reconciliation that followed was the key to Erdoğan's rise
to power.

The hapless Menderes, though, was the first victim of the
contradictions of capitalism: he was a bourgeois politician
who failed because he alienated part of the bourgeoisie, the
economic interests that were ascendant, if not yet dominant.
He was doomed ultimately by the clash between agrarian
economics and the dynamics of a rising industrial capitalism.
The coup that ended both his rule and his life ushered in a new
institutional order that was better adapted to the demands of
industrial capitalist development, but it too soon faced a new
class challenge – this time between labour and capital – that
brought new convulsions.

Menderes was overthrown in the coup of 27 May 1960. The
military conspirators were a group of colonels, majors and
captains who defied the chain of command; they arrested the
chief of the general staff together with the president, the prime
minister and several cabinet ministers. They had no common
programme or idea: some wanted to institute permanent
military rule while others, who eventually prevailed, wanted
to return to parliamentary rule. When Turkish radio listeners
tuned in on 27 May, they heard the deep, hoarse voice of
Colonel Alparslan Türkeş, who read out the announcement
of the coup makers. Türkeş was the strongman of the junta,
and he led the faction that wanted to keep power permanently.
A native of Cyprus, he had a long history of involvement in
far-right, pan-Turkic politics; he was a fascist who dreamt of
uniting all Turkic-speaking peoples, from Turkey to eastern
China. Türkeş and 13 other junta members lost the power
struggle that ensued and were exiled to diplomatic postings
abroad. But Türkeş was soon allowed to return, and he

became the leader of the fascist movement and eventually deputy prime minister in the 1970s. The party he founded, the Nationalist Action Party, formed part of the right-wing, Nationalist Front coalition governments in the 1970s, and the party's youth militia, the so-called Grey Wolves, protected by the state, assassinated left-wing intellectuals, journalists, students and trade union leaders with impunity.

Even though the officers who staged the coup in 1960 did not share a common ideology or any coherent vision, and most of them probably had only a vague, if any, understanding of the socioeconomic dynamics that had set the stage for the unravelling of the conservative government, their action nonetheless answered to and reflected the general sense of frustration that had spread among broad swathes of Turkish society by the end of the 1950s. Middle-class radicals had come to view Menderes and his liberal populism as a threat to Atatürk's legacy of secularism. Menderes vehemently denied that he was a 'counter-revolutionary', and held the charge that the Kemalist 'revolution' was endangered to be unfounded and utterly ridiculous. 'Is not my personality insurance enough that the revolution is in safe hands?'[6] he retorted when confronted by a critical journalist. He saw himself as a modern person, and remarked that he, unlike his predecessor, the last prime minister of the Kemalist era Şemsettin Günaltay, was not a mullah. He claimed that the 'revolution' was in safer hands now that he, and not a mullah, was prime minister. Menderes had a point in so far as militant secularism had already been abandoned during the Kemalist CHPs last years in power, but the perception that he was a counter-revolutionary nonetheless contributed to undermining his position, as middle-class radicals mounted a vocal opposition against him in the columns of the press that they dominated, to which Menderes unwisely responded with harsh repression. But it was not an impulse to restore militant secularism that motivated the coup, as the standard history claims. It was triggered by the violence and oppression that the ousted prime minister had unleashed, and which lent legitimacy to the coup among the urban classes, the middle class and the working class, that had suffered from Menderes' repression.

What finally undid Menderes was that he forfeited the support of the United States. He made his last, extended foreign trip as prime minister to the US at the end of 1959. The trip proved to be a major disappointment for Menderes, who had hoped to secure a financial aid package from the Americans. The US president, Dwight D. Eisenhower, gave Menderes a portrait of himself as gift during a brief meeting at the White House, but not the money he had sought. Menderes left the White House clinging to nothing else but his wrapped gift. Clearly, the policy makers in Washington had concluded that the Turkish ruler was a lost cause. Upon his return to Turkey, Menderes dug himself deeper into the hole by announcing that he was going to visit the Soviet Union in July 1960 to ask for Soviet aid instead. It was a geopolitical U-turn that showed how desperate and irrational the conservative prime minister had become. Menderes was the quintessential Cold Warrior, and one whom the Soviets were hardly going to trust and help out, not least since Turkey was a major pillar of the US policy of containment of the Soviet Union. Menderes' communist-bashing had bored even the American audiences he addressed, but the United States was unlikely to acquiesce to any Turkish 'opening' to the Soviet Union. Menderes never made it to Moscow. In his coup announcement on 27 May

1960, Colonel Türkeş, not coincidentally, vowed that the junta that had overthrown Menderes was going to respect Turkey's alliance obligations as a member of NATO.

There is no evidence that the coup was coordinated with the United States, but the coup makers must at the very least have felt encouraged by the treatment that Menderes had received in Washington a few months earlier. The history of Turkish coups suggests that two preconditions must be in place if a coup is to succeed: first, a social and political context in which the dominant (or ascendant) class interests are frustrated and call for the overthrow of the elected government; second, the explicit or tacit benediction of the United States. As we will see later, the coup in 1980 was the perfect example: it answered to the needs of the bourgeoisie and it was encouraged by the United States. In 2016, when a faction of the military failed to overthrow Erdoğan, one of the preconditions was in place, but not the second: the attempt enjoyed tacit US benediction, but it crucially lacked a class dimension, indeed a social base, which in part accounts for why it did not succeed. All preceding coups – in 1960, 1971, 1980 and 1997 – were grounded in class realities, but this is generally overlooked in accounts of Turkish history.

Standard history depicts the 1960 coup as restoring the power of the bureaucracy over the people, after a ten-year parenthesis. Indeed, after 1960, a new constitutional order was put in place designed to curb the power of the elected government. The constitution adopted in 1961 introduced a number of checks and balances: a constitutional court, a council of state, a national security council which officialized the military's right to interfere in politics, and a two-chamber parliament, composed of an elected assembly and a senate whose majority was elected, but where a quota was reserved for the president to fill out with appointed senators. The new order did reassert the power of the state and the bureaucracy, but now within the context of a capitalist order: the bureaucracy was aligned with and served ascendant industrial interests. A cornerstone of the post-1960 system was the State Planning Organization, which nursed a private industrial sector that prospered by producing for a protected internal market. By the mid 1960s, Turkey even boasted an automobile industry, even though it relied almost entirely on imported components. The Anadol became something of a new national symbol, like the Hindustani automobiles in India, when it rolled out onto the roads in 1966. Anadol's engine was English-made, but its fibreglass body offered little security on Turkish roads.

The industrial planning policies enacted at this time were those that the nascent industry had been calling for since the mid 1950s. The new, post-coup order was ultimately designed to deal with the minority status of the urban classes – led by the industrial bourgeoisie – in a country that was still dominated by a peasant population but where industrial interests were ascendant. As we have seen, popular will had worked against the interests of industrial capital, because electoral arithmetic had encouraged, indeed compelled, the Menderes government to dismiss the demands of industry and privilege the interests of the majority, the rural base. The post-1960 technocratic system was devised to ensure that the popular will did not interfere with the conduct of the economy; in that respect, what was put in place in Turkey during this period was not dissimilar to the present institutional framework of the European Union: the governing logic behind the European Monetary Union, the independent European Central Bank and the stability pact that circumscribes public spending is directed toward very much the same end – ensuring that democracy does not interfere with economics.

Yet a new pattern of conflict soon emerged that revealed the internal contradictions of the new institutional framework. The growth of the industrial sector brought with it a conflict between labour and capital that upended the dynamic that had existed until 1960. Before 1960, the working class had been small and was included, in a subordinate role, in the urban coalition that tried to assert itself against the rural majority; the defining class conflict was not yet between labour and capital, and industrial interests had thus not objected to the rights that labour was accorded in the new regime. But during the course of the 1960s Turkey became 'normalized', with the emergence of the normal patterns of class conflict of an industrial economy. For the industrial bourgeoisie – and for the state bureaucracy that supervised the economy in the best interests of capital – it now became imperative to keep the working class in check. And religion was deemed to be the best antidote to socialism.

Antidote to the Left

Hamdullah Suphi Tanrıöver was a prominent member of the establishment during the one-party rule of the CHP. He served as education minister, an ambassador and a parliamentarian. In 1946, Tanrıöver presented a motion in parliament calling for the reintroduction of religious education into the school curriculum. Under Atatürk, all religious education had ceased, but after his death in 1938 his party quickly moved to abandon the anti-religious militancy that had been a defining feature of the Kemalist era. The need to break with this militancy appeared all the more urgent with the onset of the Cold War and the fear that the Soviet Union was scheming to promote socialism in Turkey. Tanrıöver justified his proposal to restart religious education by appealing to the need to ensure that young people acquired 'a moral strength to withstand the threat of communism'. However, this hysterical anti-communism – it held reformist social democracy to be as subversive as Marxism-Leninism – was not only an expression of bourgeois class interests; it was as much, perhaps even more so, culturally motivated. Conservatives dreaded communism, indeed leftist ideas in general, as the ultimate expression of a modernity that in their view threatened traditional culture and its values.

Radical secularism was officially declared a dead letter at the seventh congress of the ruling CHP the following year, 1947, the same year that President Harry S. Truman announced that the United States was going to extend financial and military aid to Greece and Turkey as part of the containment of Soviet expansion. The CHP congress officially recognized that cultural and religious reforms could not be imposed from above, and that only such reforms as were in line with popular wishes could be implemented. The militant stance toward Islam was abandoned. The radical wing of the party was purged. Two years earlier, in 1945, the radical faction had proposed to reform Islam, envisioning much more far-reaching reforms than those the Kemalist regime had contemplated, let alone sought to implement. They demanded that the Quran be translated into 'pure Turkish'. This was the new language that Atatürk had promoted, in which the Arabic and Persian words that dominated Ottoman Turkish had been cleansed and replaced with purportedly 'pure' Turkish words of supposedly Central Asian origin. In fact, in many cases, words deemed to sound 'pure' were simply invented. This demand for translation was an affront to the pious, as Islamic tradition holds that to translate the Quran, which is held to be the word of God, amounts to sacrilege. The CHP radicals also wanted to turn places of worship into 'people's halls', and called for a prohibition on all religious attires. The radicals were unaware that they were wholly out of touch with the times, which, with the perceived threat from the left, called for religious restoration not the extension of Atatürk's cultural revolution.

The 1947 CHP congress thus called for the reintroduction of voluntary religious instruction in elementary schools; it decided that the imam schools – where future preachers in mosques are educated, and which had been shut down in 1930 officially because of a lack of interest – should be reopened. It was also decided that the public should once again be allowed access to religious shrines and tombs. Finally, the ruling CHP instructed the government to make foreign currency available for those citizens who wished to make the *hajj*, the pilgrimage to Mecca and Medina, which is one of the five pillars of the Muslim faith. But these were only the first steps; not coincidentally, the expansion of religious education picked up from the 1960s onward, when class conflict hardened.

When the conservative Justice Party came to power in 1965, the imam schools numbered 65; two years later there were 84, and the number of pupils attending them had more than doubled, from 13,000 to 30,000. The expansion of the Quran courses, provided by the State Directorate of Religious Affairs to school children after school hours, was even more dramatic: at the beginning of the 1930s, there were only nine of these in the whole of Turkey; in 1960 they numbered 658, and by 1990 they totalled 4,420, with more than 1 million children attending. In parallel with the expansion of religious education, members of the previously shunned Islamic fraternities – which had been forced underground during Atatürk's rule – were welcomed into the state bureaucracy where they eventually became entrenched. The State Planning Organization (DPT) became a stronghold of the powerful Islamic Nakshibendi fraternity. Turgut Özal, who was a member of the fraternity, was appointed undersecretary of the DPT. As the top bureaucrat in Turkey, he made sure that the doors of the bureaucracy were flung wide open for his fellow Nakshibendis. Özal's career is an excellent illustration of how the Turkish state establishment, the Islamic movement, right-wing authoritarianism and neoliberal economics are intertwined. In 1977, Özal stood for election to parliament as a candidate for the Islamist National Salvation Party (MSP). He failed in that bid, but returned in grand style three years later, when the right-wing military junta that had taken power on 12 September 1980 appointed him deputy prime minister in charge of the economy. In that capacity, Özal, who was given a free hand, executed a neoliberal revolution in the style of Margaret Thatcher and Ronald Reagan. He subsequently founded the Motherland Party (ANAP), which styled itself liberal-conservative and won the election in 1983 that only politicians who had been approved by the military junta were allowed to contest. He was elected president in 1989 and died of a heart attack in 1993. As a pious Muslim and a neoliberal who admired America, Özal became the darling of policy and opinion makers in the United States. But Özal was no democrat.

The generals who handed the economy over to him in 1980 had imprisoned all political leaders, dissolved their parties, and barred them from re-entering politics. Eventually though, the old political leadership began to reassert itself and the question of whether the former party leaders should be allowed to return to politics was put to a referendum in 1987. Özal, who was then prime minister, campaigned vigorously against lifting the ban imposed by the military junta, but lost. When his conservative party subsequently lost its majority in parliament, Özal, who had secured his elevation to the presidency before that, called for the introduction of a presidential system that would concentrate executive powers in the president, as compensation for his party's declining electoral fortunes. Back in the 1970s, other leaders of the Turkish right had called for the rule of a *caudillo*, as a way of ensuring that the left was kept at bay; indeed, as we have seen, the conservative Menderes had made a failed bid to impose himself as a *caudillo*. But it was Erdoğan, a Nakshibendi and neoliberal like Özal, who was going to succeed where all other right-wing leaders before him had failed, when he secured the approval of the voters for presidential rule in a referendum in 2017.

In the 1960s and 1970s, a central role in manning the ideological barricades against the rising tide of the left was played by a group of conservatives who came together in what they styled 'The hearth of the intellectuals'. This was a deeply influential group of right-wing thinkers who advised and instructed the parties of the right, as well as the military, to advance Islamization as an antidote to the left. They produced what they called a 'Turkish-Islamic synthesis', an amalgamation of Turkish nationalism and Islam. This 'synthesis' became the ideological blueprint for the military junta that took power in

1980. The conservative intellectuals of the 'hearth' believed that the challenge of the left could only be defeated if Islam was given a much more prominent place in the ideology of the state, and they served as bridge-builders between the 'secular' right and the Islamic movement. They encouraged and helped bring about the amalgamation of the right into a united, nationalist-Islamist front against the left. The bourgeois order of Turkey has been well served by the combination of Islam and nationalism. As one parliamentarian of the governing conservative Justice Party stated in the late 1960s: 'To give Turkish children a religious and national consciousness, to teach them to be Turkish and Islamic, is the way to ensure that leftism is neutralized.'[7] However, the right was to be challenged by a social democratic politician who believed that the left and popular religiosity should be reconciled, and who aspired to bridge the divide between the progressives and the pious masses that had handed the populist right a monopoly on power.

CHAPTER FIVE

Social Democratic Hope

Portrait of an Aristocratic Radical

A different kind of politician emerged around the Western world during the 1960s: Robert F. Kennedy in the United States, Pierre Trudeau in Canada, Jean-Jacques Servan-Schreiber in France, Olof Palme in Sweden. They were young, progressive and charismatic. They all hailed from privileged social backgrounds, were endowed with a rich cultural capital, and had been educated at elite schools. They shared an ambition to democratize and modernize their respective societies. They inspired hope among the broad masses. The Swedish historian Henrik Berggren, biographer of Olof Palme, the Swedish social democratic leader, calls them 'aristocratic radicals'. Bülent Ecevit was the Turkish aristocratic radical. Born in 1925, like Robert Kennedy, he also came from a privileged social and cultural background and had received an elite education. His star began to shine in the mid 1960s, and he became the great progressive hope of his country. Like both Kennedy and Palme, with whom he developed a friendship, Ecevit was a powerful orator. His rise, and that of social democracy under his charismatic leadership, defined Turkish politics from the late 1960s to the end of the 1970s. But it also triggered a violent right-wing reaction: fascist death squads killed thousands of leftists during the 1970s, and the

Figure 4   Social democratic hope: the centre-left leader Bülent
Ecevit, here speaking from the back of a truck at a rally in the early
1970s, broke the hold of the right on the people. He established a
unique rapport with the popular masses.

military finished the job in the coup of 1980 that crushed the
left once and for all.

Ecevit is to date the only social democrat to have been
prime minister of Turkey. He was elected to parliament in
1957, and entered the government in 1961 as labour minister.
In 1966, he became party secretary of the CHP. In 1972,
Ecevit unseated the man who had been Atatürk's lieutenant
and the leader of CHP since 1938, the former president İsmet
İnönü, and was elected party leader. Ecevit engineered the
centrist CHP's radical shift to the left. In 1976, the party was
officially rebranded as democratic leftist, and was on the way
to establishing itself as Turkey's major political force. A social
and democratic transformation beckoned in the country, like
the one that social democratic parties had engineered in the
former right-wing dictatorships of Greece, Spain and Portugal.

But that was not allowed to be repeated in Turkey. When Ecevit died in 2006, the *Guardian* commented that 'He might have come to be thought of as a great social democratic reformer', but that 'his career was in many ways blown off course by the tensions of Turkey's domestic political scene', and that the right-wing parties had 'pulled out every stop to exclude Ecevit from power'.[1] Indeed, as we will see in the following chapter, Ecevit was caught in the cross-fire of the interests he challenged: the right-wing parties, the military, big business and the United States.

Yet he nonetheless notched up a number of political victories: as labour minister in 1963 he secured collective bargaining rights and the right to strike for industrial workers. When he was asked by reporters many years later, in 2000, to rate his greatest political achievement, he replied that it was the laws that accorded the workers their rights. One reporter expressed his surprise; he had expected that Ecevit would have singled out his decision as prime minister in 1974 to order the Turkish military to invade Cyprus in response to an attempt to unite the island with Greece, or his role in the late 1990s in securing Turkish membership negotiations with the European Union, or the handover of Abdullah Öcalan, the leader of the militant Kurdistan Workers' Party (PKK) to Turkey by American agents in 1998, which had been greeted as a huge Turkish success by nationalist opinion. 'No,' said Ecevit, 'for me, giving the workers trade union rights is more important than all of that, because I am a leftist.'[2] Nothing, though, is left today of the accomplishment of which Ecevit was so proud.

The right-wing military junta that took power in 1980 removed all of the rights that had been accorded to workers, as it imposed a neoliberal strait-jacket on the country. Erdoğan and his 'Islamic' conservatives are the heirs of the military: they have been as faithful servants of capital as the generals were, maintaining the labour-hostile order. Turkey holds the world record in fatal work-related accidents, and Turkish workers are left defenceless as labour unions, although no longer banned as they were during the junta years, have in practice been rendered powerless by government regulations and the pressures of the employers. The numbers are striking and reveal the extent to which labour conditions have degenerated since neoliberalism was imposed on Turkey in 1980: then, Turkey counted 2.2 million workers; of these, 2 million were unionized. It was not least in order to break this labour power that the military staged its coup. In 2017, the number of workers had swelled to 13.6 million, but of these only 1.6 million were unionized. While 90 per cent of workers were unionized in 1980, today 90 per cent are not. Ninety-five per cent of the labour force work without a collective bargaining agreement. The situation is worst in the construction sector, which is the principal engine of the Turkish economy and which also accounts for most of the fatal work-related accidents; less than 3 per cent of the workers in this sector are organized.

It was not coincidental that late in life Ecevit felt the need to emphasize that he was a leftist: in the final stage of his political career he had ceased to embody any kind of leftist hope, and had come to be seen as just another mainstream politician who served rather than challenged the system, as he had done in the 1960s and 1970s. But to judge by his assurance that he was a leftist, and that his proudest achievement had been to secure the workers' rights, it was as the man who had challenged the capitalist system that he wanted to be remembered. We certainly have little use for the Ecevit of the 1990s. It is his pre-1980 legacy that is worth revisiting: his writings and activism from the 1950s to the late 1970s show the way for the left today in Turkey, and perhaps elsewhere as well.

In the 1960s and 1970s, Ecevit looked to Western Europe, and in particular to the Scandinavian social democratic countries, for inspiration. Today, however, it is the far right that is ascendant in those countries, while the working class and the social democratic parties have drifted apart from each other.[3] Now, it is progressives in Europe and in the United States that have insights to gain from the example of Ecevit. What he set out to do was reconcile the left and the people; he showed how the cultural divisions that had disabled the left in Turkey – and which the right was so skilful at exploiting, just like the populist far right in Europe and the American right today – could be transcended. Crucially, he disagreed with those progressives who held that modernity and popular religiosity were in opposition and that the pious were by definition reactionaries. That, he pointed out, was the 'historical mistake' of the Turkish leftists, and he exhorted them to recognize that 'the pious can also be progressives'. When he secured the left's only election victory in Turkey to date – in the general election of 1977 his democratic leftist CHP received nearly 42 per cent of the votes – Ecevit made history. Scant, if any, attention is paid to that history in the standard narratives on Turkey, yet the destruction of Turkish social democracy goes a long way in accounting for why the country is still authoritarian. Nevertheless, the rise of social democracy in the 1970s showed that there is a way out of the impasse, and that Turkey is not sociologically fated to remain right-wing and authoritarian.

Bülent Ecevit's family history accounts for his unique ability to transcend Turkey's secular-Islamic cultural divide. That may seem improbable at first glance: he hailed from an elite, even 'aristocratic' background. How could that possibly have contributed to the making of a populist-leftist leader who was able to establish a rapport with the pious masses? The answer is that Ecevit was endowed with a cultural capital that anchored him in the Ottoman religious world, and which sensitized him to the power of religious feelings; he was from an early age pulled toward Islamic, but also Hindu, mysticism. Men of religion dominated Ecevit's lineage on both his mother's side and his father's; little wonder then that for him Islam was, as he said, a 'light'.[4] Ecevit was not in the habit of praying in the mosque, but it is he, not the religion-mongering right-wing politicians, who comes across as truly pious. Erdoğan is known never to miss the weekly Friday prayer; in the 1980s the right-wing military dictator Kenan Evren used to wave the Quran during his public rallies, and boasted that he was the son of a mullah. For his part, Ecevit found nothing sincere in the Turkish right-wing politicians' displays of 'religiosity'; he pointed out that this was only a smoke-screen that served to hide the nature of the class relations and the system of exploitation that the right upheld.

Ecevit's father was a medical doctor who dabbled in politics, serving for two terms as a member of parliament for the ruling CHP; his mother was a painter. His parents were sufficiently well-off to be able to send their son to the elite Robert College in Istanbul, Turkey's premier high school, where education was given in English. But what was more important for the formation of the future radical-populist politician was the cultural capital they passed on to him from their own parents and grandparents. Ecevit's parents were certainly members of the elite of the young Turkish republic, but that is not what makes his background remarkable; it is the family heritage from the preceding generations that sets him apart as an 'aristocrat'. Formally, there was no hereditary aristocracy in the Ottoman Empire, but nonetheless on his mother's side Ecevit's elite pedigree reached back to the most prominent milieus of the Ottoman *ancien régime*. His maternal grandfather, Hacı Emin Pasha, was one of the highest Ottoman religious dignitaries, a sheikh-ul-Islam of the holy cities Mecca and Medina. This maternal grandfather's father in turn was an Ottoman general, and the aide-de-camp of Sultan Abdülhamid II. Ecevit's paternal grandfather Mustafa Şükrü Efendi was a respected religious scholar who taught in mosques and in preacher seminars in the Ottoman capital.

But Ecevit inherited more than a rich cultural capital: he was also heir to a vast fortune, even though nothing in his frugal lifestyle – books were the only things he ever cared about possessing – hinted at the family fortune that had been bequeathed to him. Ecevit had inherited his maternal grandfather's properties in what is now Saudi Arabia – an inheritance that was estimated to be worth an astounding 2 billion US dollars in 2005. A year before he died, Ecevit, who had no children, donated his Saudi properties and financial assets to the Turkish State Directorate of Religious Affairs, with the instruction that they be used to provide for Turkish pilgrims making the *haj* to Saudi Arabia. Until then, little had been known in Turkey about the Ottoman elite lineage of Ecevit, and nothing at all about his family fortune.

Ecevit himself was for a long time unaware of one part of his ethnic heritage. He was over 40 when he discovered that he was of Kurdish origin on his father's side. He revealed this to the public more than three decades later, in 2004, two years before his death, explaining that he had discovered his Kurdish roots when he travelled to the province in central Anatolia from where his father hailed, and there paid a visit to the tomb of his grandfather. 'That was when I learned about it, when I saw his tomb',[5] he recalled. He discovered that his paternal grandfather, Mustafa Şükrü Efendi, was also known by a family name,[6] 'Kürtzade', which means 'of Kurdish lineage'. Neither Ecevit's father nor his grandfather had ever mentioned this fact, since, as Ecevit said, 'Back then, such distinctions were not important.'[7] The Ecevits are in no way unique in this regard, and many other Turks have similarly stumbled upon previously unknown family origins. The invention of a 'pure' Turkish nation after the founding of the republic in 1923 had made every reference to other ethnic roots dangerous, not only in public, but also domestically; it was common for people to choose not to divulge their origins even to their own family, as was the case with Ecevit's father.

I referred earlier to the childhood memory of the leading Kemalist leftist intellectual İlhan Selçuk, who recalled how his parents had not dared to continue to speak Greek, their native language, at home after the government in the 1930s decreed that every citizen must speak Turkish. But such oblivion is not only imposed or self-imposed, it is also a consequence of the chaos that accompanied the creation of Turkey, when millions were displaced from their places of birth; as a result, many people in Turkey today know little or nothing about their origins, and assume that they are 'pure' Turkish. Existential traumas and tragedies have been triggered when people who had taken it for granted that they were Turks have discovered that they were in fact of Kurdish or, even more unsettling, of Armenian origin. In one such particularly tragic case, a young conscript committed suicide upon learning about the Armenian origin of his family during his military service. He had applied to train as a pilot, but the military records revealed that his grandmother was a survivor of the Armenian genocide who, like countless other Ottoman Armenian girls, had been abducted and converted to Islam. This disqualified him – and every other descendant of the woman – from sensitive positions in the Turkish state, such as becoming a pilot in the air force.

The case of Ecevit's paternal grandfather, the Kurdish religious scholar, is doubly interesting, because he subsumed both of the identities – the ethnic and the religious – that have tormented and disabled the Turkish left. Yet while Ecevit was well equipped, thanks to his family lineage, to empathize with the pious, he could never similarly assume his ethnic heritage, of which he had grown up being unaware; he never really understood the ethnic sentiment that powered the Kurds' aspirations. He seems to have thought that since his own ethnic Kurdish heritage was of little consequence for how he viewed himself, neither should it matter – at least not in political terms – for other Turkish citizens who shared the same ethnic background. He did not deny the Kurdish identity, but he failed to recognize that social and economic reforms alone would not satisfy the Kurds, and that a solution to the ethnic question would also require some form of political recognition of Kurdish identity. We will soon see how this failure limited the impact of his vision of a social democracy for Turkey that he hoped to anchor in the popular, but heterogeneous, culture of Anatolia.

Ecevit's biography stands out as strikingly unusual in almost every respect: before entering politics, he worked as a journalist, in Turkey but also in the United States. In 1954 he received a fellowship from the US State Department to work as a visiting journalist at the *Winston-Salem Journal and Sentinel* in North Carolina. As a politician, Ecevit would fall out with the United States, but in the 1950s he was still conventionally pro-American in the way many progressives in Europe and in the Third World were at the time, as America was seen as a force for development and emancipation. Ecevit made a few unpleasant discoveries though, during his stay in Winston-Salem. He was shocked by the racism of the South, and wrote a highly critical article about it. To its credit, the *Winston-Salem Journal and Sentinel* published Ecevit's piece, but only after he had left, since the editor wanted to spare him any angry reactions from the townsfolk. Initially, Ecevit was not a political writer but an art critic; he was also a founder of one of Turkey's first modern-art galleries. According to one leading Turkish painter, it was thanks to Ecevit that the capital Ankara, a cultural backwater, had enjoyed a lively cultural life at the beginning of the 1950s. But the gallery, Helikon, was shut down by the authorities in 1955, after the government unleashed a pogrom that targeted the Greek minority in Istanbul; the Greek name of the art gallery had made it appear suspicious, and Ecevit was briefly detained. That was not to be his last encounter with the prisons of the Turkish state. After the right-wing military junta seized power in 1980, Ecevit defied the decrees that forbade him to write and talk about politics or to give interviews to foreign media, and he was twice sent to prison.

In 1946, Ecevit had taken up a position as second secretary at the office of the press attaché at the Turkish embassy in London. His years in London in the late 1940s were to have a formative impact on his political views. Back in Turkey in 1951, he wrote that 'London is not a city to be visited and looked at, but a city to be lived and experienced.'[8] He was both struck and repelled by the arrogance of the aristocratic youth who walked around with their 'noses in the air', but what he experienced above all in London was how 'a people that had discovered societal consciousness and solidarity together was able to meet and overcome the hardships after the war in a shared spirit of social justice'.[9] Ecevit and his wife were moved by the sense of solidarity that British society displayed at the time, and by the sacrifices people made for the sake of the common good. He was impressed by 'English socialism', by the reduction of income differences, and by what he described – in one his columns in *Ulus*, the newspaper owned by CHP where he took up a position upon his return from London – as the crumbling of the class walls. He decided that he wanted to implement what he had witnessed in England in Turkey, adapting English socialism to Turkish conditions.

This was an unlikely career choice. Ecevit was an introverted, bookish person who kept his distance from others. No one who knew him before he entered politics would have expected that the shy young intellectual who disliked socializing and preferred the company of books was going to turn into a charismatic tribune, a powerful orator who established an emotionally charged rapport with the popular masses. In his early years, Ecevit seemed more likely to be remembered as a poet, and throughout his life he remained a man of letters. 'There can be few other prime ministers anywhere who, coming out of a press conference and noticing that a journalist was holding a new book on the 17th century English poet John Donne, would have asked to borrow it',[10] noted his *Guardian* obituary. He began composing poetry in high school. Above all, he excelled as a translator of poetry: he was only 16 when his translation of Rabindranath Tagore was published, and he subsequently translated T.S. Eliot and Ezra Pound, among others. But it was with Tagore and his Hindu mysticism that Ecevit was infatuated. While working at the office of the Turkish press attaché in London, he took the opportunity to follow courses in Sanskrit and Bengali at the School of Oriental and African Studies. Later in life, he would still regret that the work burden at the embassy had prevented him from finishing his studies and mastering Sanskrit.

Ecevit was to be derided as a 'romantic poet' by his political opponents. He certainly stood apart as a political leader: his predecessors as CHP leaders, Atatürk and İnönü, were battled-hardened military men, while his arch-rival during the 1960s and the 1970s, the conservative politician Demirel, was an engineer. Some, both to the left and to the right, held that Ecevit was too much of an intellectual and a 'dreamer' to succeed in politics. In fact, Ecevit's greatest 'flaw' was that he never internalized the capitalist system; we will soon see how the bourgeoisie punished and destroyed him for his refusal to abide by capitalist imperatives. As 'poetic' as he was, he was tough-minded and determined, while on the flip side, he could also be stubborn and insensitive to the views of others. He was a loner. Ecevit was an intellectual who never identified with the intellectuals of his country; on the contrary, he identified them as part of Turkey's problem, and as a politician he always kept them at arms' length. He preferred the company of peasants and workers and said that he felt closer to the lower classes than to the members of the elite from which he hailed. Of course, the masses idolized him, at least during the years

Figure 5   Ecevit in his characteristic Jeff cap, worn by the peasants in Anatolia. Ecevit was an 'aristocratic' intellectual who cultivated a folksy appearance.

that he embodied the hope of change, while his intellectual peers were not predisposed to be awed by him, and indeed often disagreed with him. His statements in one of the last interviews he gave spoke of bitterness: he complained that the intellectuals had never understood what he tried to do and that they had laughed at his ideas.

But Ecevit was always a harsh critic of the Turkish intelligentsia; he argued that one reason why progressive, leftist ideas had not been accepted by society was the haughty manners of the educated, of those who thought of themselves as 'enlightened' and progressive and who did little to hide their contempt for ordinary people. The Turkish word for intellectual, *aydın*, literally means to be 'enlightened', but it can also be translated as 'luminary'; it refers to something broader than an academic or thinker. Academics and thinkers are not necessarily 'enlightened'. Conversely, a Turkish *aydın* did not need to be a thinker or writer; he or she was of course usually a professor, a writer or a journalist, but a rich businessman or a high-ranking bureaucrat could also qualify as a 'luminary'. In class terms, the word simply designated bourgeois radicals. What was required was to have received a modern education and to have a 'modern' outlook; it used to be assumed that such people stood above the ordinary, uneducated men and women and that they were inherently 'progressive' because they were educated. Those who qualified as 'luminaries' certainly themselves took this for granted.

So what Ecevit really took issue with was the bourgeois radicals, the pretentious elite progressives, who had done the left such a disservice with their contempt for the uncouth peasants and workers they were supposedly going to 'enlighten'. In an article Ecevit penned in the daily *Ulus* in 1956, titled 'The Problem of the "Luminary"', he sketched a damning portrait of the 'enlightened' bourgeois of the period. But the article also has a resonance in our own time; what Ecevit had to say about his country's elitist 'progressives' could just as well be said about their equivalents in the United States and in many European countries today. Their reactions to the working-class vote for Donald Trump and his like are moralizing and judgmental rather than informed by empathy. Ecevit's words speak to the present:

> Democracy is a system of government that teaches humility to the intellectuals (or the 'enlightened') and, through this humility, teaches them to heed the concerns of the majority, and to interest themselves in their concerns. These principles can only be realized through democracy, so that,

even within the poorest neighbourhoods that lie along his path, the intellectual will grow accustomed to going door to door and preaching the benefits of progressive thought and open-mindedness.[11]

Of course, this is precisely the problem today: the poorest neighbourhoods no longer lie along the path of American and European progressives; they rarely, if ever, show up there. Lawrence Summers, a former Secretary of the Treasury under the Democrat Bill Clinton, self-critically reflected on the fact that he had never travelled to the industrial wastelands of the United States during his tenure in government. It was Hillary Clinton's undoing in the US presidential election of 2016 that she came across as the ultimate embodiment of the arrogant 'progressive' elite, not least after her remark that half of Donald Trump's supporters belonged in a 'basket of deplorables'. Clinton had of course every reason and the right to condemn racist, sexist, homophobic and Islamophobic expressions; but she also needed to demonstrate that she recognized that what is helping to bring out these demons is unbounded capitalism. The 'enlightened' American political elite was shocked when the support of working-class voters helped Trump win the presidency, but they seem to have little appreciation of their own responsibility for the distress of the working class or of how that distress has led to its turn to the right. In so far as the centre-left has embraced neoliberalism since the 1980s, it also bears a responsibility for the rise of the populist right today.

There are nonetheless 'progressives' today who show outright contempt for the lower classes, the uneducated, the working class, who they hold to be 'reactionary'. A particularly ostentatious example was provided by the leading French think-tank Terra Nova, which has had a significant impact on the policies of the French Socialist Party in recent years. In a study from 2011, Terra Nova concluded that the working class was a lost cause for the socialists, because 'workers nowadays position themselves primarily in function of their cultural values – and these values are profoundly anchored to the right'.[12] The 'socialist' think-tank advised the Socialist Party – whose free market economic policies have alienated its former working-class base – not to try to win back the working class, and instead focus on the young, the multicultural and all those in society who embrace modernity and globalization, on those the French call 'bobos', the bohemian-bourgeois class, the hipsters. This is just the kind of bourgeois cultural arrogance that Ecevit indicted in his article about the problem of the Turkish 'luminaries'. Contrary to Ecevit, for whom self-professed progressives should be 'going door to door and preaching the benefits of progressive thought and open-mindedness' in the poor neighbourhoods, thinkers of what passes as socialism in Europe today claim that there is no point in doing that. The French geographer Christophe Guilluy has made a striking analysis: he argues that the 'progressive' bourgeoisie, the 'bobos' who back globalization in the name of tolerance, openness and multiculturalism, have played a key role in sustaining and legitimating neoliberalism by stigmatizing its critics as 'reactionaries' or 'racists'.[13] This, he says, applies to all Western societies. The working-class neighbourhoods are being abandoned to the far right.

Ecevit did the opposite: he knocked on the doors of the working class. When he became party secretary of the CHP in 1966, he cancelled the proms the party had used to host for the bourgeoisie of the capital and took to 'walking around the

suburbs of Ankara', as he said. He instructed the party organization to 'seek out the people', instead of mingling with the
bourgeoisie; party representatives who had previously been
expected to attend their party's proms were now sent out to
drink tea and make small talk with workers, low-paid functionaries, shopkeepers and housewives in the working-class
districts of Ankara. This was a way of fighting the prejudices and
stereotypes that informed how Turkey's 'luminaries' viewed
the lower classes. In his 1956 article, Ecevit had described their
attitudes; the article takes the form of an imaginary encounter
on a public bus between a haughty member of the bourgeois
elite and an impoverished, uneducated man of the people:

> He's either a professor in a department, a rich businessman,
> or a high-ranking bureaucrat. With his clothes, the way he
> walks and talks, he's a complete 'Westerner'. He is one of
> this country's 'luminaries', one of our 'select few'. On the
> bus, after surveying from head to toe a poorly dressed man
> with a patched shirt who sits across from him, he will turn
> to the man next to him: 'There you have it', he'll say, 'that
> man sitting across from us is our destiny. If democracy is
> brought to a country where 80 per cent of the population
> are illiterate, that's exactly what our country will look like!

Ecevit noted that the 'luminaries' had not managed to avoid
the feelings of superiority that come from occupying the head
of the table, and he doubted that they themselves believed
in the 'progressive' ideas they professed. He wrote that 'they
have not been able to summon enough faith to face self-
sacrifice or danger for the sake of disseminating those ideas'.
His conclusion was prophetic and has a striking relevancy

for democracy's prospects in today's world: 'If democracy is brought to a country where 80 per cent of the intelligentsia are either haughty and spineless, lazy and dyspeptic, or fearful and lacking in belief, *this* is what our country will become!'

Turkey has stayed right-wing authoritarian, not because the people are 'backward', but partly because the progressives' contempt for them has contributed to the disabling of the left. And that may be what the future has in store in other countries around the world as well, if self-professed progressives persist in writing off the people as hopelessly reactionary.

Ecevit's seminal article also exhibits an awareness that disseminating progressive ideas is fraught with danger, and that progressives will need to 'summon enough faith to face self-sacrifice'. Indeed, Ecevit's father warned him about the dangers he courted and advised him to be soft-spoken in his writings, without however making concessions: 'Socialists in this country are going to face the slander that they are communists for another half-century', Fahri Ecevit presciently predicted in a letter to his son.[14] It was as if he sensed what lay ahead: a decade after those words were written, when in the mid 1960s Ecevit had taken the lead in rebranding the CHP as left of centre, the right responded with the slogan 'Left of the centre is the path to Moscow.'

That was sure to incite hatred and summon up demons: in the eyes of the masses, communism equalled Godlessness, and nothing could be more dangerous than being seen as 'Godless' in a deeply religious society like Turkey. That was precisely the popular prejudice that Ecevit had to overcome if he was going to win the people for the cause of the left. He would to a large measure succeed in this endeavour, but things were also going to get much worse as he earned the trust and support of the masses, which made him so much more dangerous to the ruling class and the right. In the 1970s, the bourgeoisie came to view Ecevit as a Turkish incarnation of Salvador Allende, Chile's socialist president who was killed in the military coup of 1973. They had the same end in mind for Ecevit. Süleyman Demirel, the leader of the Turkish right, called Bülent Ecevit 'Allende Büllende'. That was certainly not innocent name-calling. Several attempts were made to assassinate Ecevit during the 1970s, and his rallies regularly came under gunfire, but he was a progressive who lived by his own words and who mustered 'enough faith to face self-sacrifice'. 'His flinty personal courage never faltered', as the *Guardian* noted in his obituary.

The Promise of an Anatolian Left

Since his London years at the end of the 1940s, when he witnessed first-hand the Labour Party's social democratic reforms, Bülent Ecevit had been a social democrat, and it seems that early on he saw himself playing a leading role both in politics and in introducing social democracy in Turkey. From the mid 1960s, social changes and the new political conjuncture that followed in their wake were to offer him the opportunity to play that role. The 1960s were the years when industrialization and urbanization truly began to reshape Turkey socially and politically; as peasants moved into the rapidly growing cities to join the swelling industrial workforce, conflict between labour and capital came to the fore, and politics became structured around a clearly distinguishable left-right dimension.

The right-wing parties clamoured for a restriction of political liberties and of the social rights that labour had been accorded in the new constitution adopted after the overthrow of the authoritarian conservative government in the coup in 1960. The right railed against the liberties in response to the ascendancy of the left and labour. As noted earlier, the socialist Labour Party of Turkey (TİP) entered parliament with 15 MPs after the 1965 general election, in which it won 3 per cent of the vote. That may seem little, but it was nonetheless a historic result. Socialist ideas were rapidly gaining traction on university campuses and among workers.

Ecevit's Republican People's Party risked being overrun in this fast-evolving social and political-ideological environment. He and others who belonged to the left wing of the CHP warned that the party faced marginalization if it did not adapt to a new era of class conflict and become a party for workers and peasants. Ecevit took the lead in the internal debates in arguing for severing the party's ties to the bourgeoisie and the landlords. Like Bernie Sanders today, who has pointed out that the Democratic Party must decide if it wants to be the party of Wall Street or of the people, Ecevit wanted the CHP to truly become a 'people's party'. For the Kemalists, the 'people' in the party name evoked a nationalist conception of a supposedly classless nation; but what Ecevit had in mind when he spoke of the people was the labouring classes, the workers and peasants, those who were excluded from power. He did not include those who laid claim to the surplus value in society and whose privileges and power violated the democratic principle of equality in his definition of the people.[15]

The CHP's traditional nationalistic definition of the people had no credibility in the new context of sharpened class conflict. The right-wing parties spoke for bourgeois interests and the emerging socialist left aspired to represent the working class; a party that pretended that these class divisions did not exist, and that it was possible to speak for the nation as a classless whole, was destined to irrelevancy. It would be left without any natural electoral constituency. The CHP had to become the agent of a 'class and an ideology', Ecevit said, if it was to avoid that fate. His convictions and his will to power combined to steer the party to the left. His internal opponents, the right-wing of the party, saw where things were headed; they accused Ecevit of wanting to refashion the CHP as a socialist party, and they were not wrong. In 1967, 43 right-wing CHP members of parliament and senators defected from the party in protest at the lurch to the left, and set up a new rightist party that was to be the junior partner of the leading conservative party. But Ecevit, who had been elected party secretary a year earlier, continued to enjoy the support of the octogenarian party leader, İnönü, at least for the time being.

It was İnönü who had first stated that the CHP was left of centre, though he was in fact anything but a leftist, and not even left of centre. İnönü had been a subordinate of Atatürk, first in the military and subsequently in government; he had succeeded him as president in 1938, resigning after he lost the first free election in 1950. He has been credited by posterity for respecting the outcome of the election, but his graceful exit from the presidency was dictated by a combination of geopolitics and class interests. By 1950, Turkey had become a front-line state in the Cold War, and was in line to join NATO. The bourgeois class interests that the Turkish state represented craved security from the threat of socialism, and İnönü realized that Turkey had to present a respectable, democratic facade in order to be accepted as a full member of the Western alliance, and enjoy full protection against socialism.

Perry Anderson describes İnönü as 'dour, pious and conservative, in appearance and outlook not unlike a somewhat less plump Turkish version of Franco'.[16] Indeed he was officially Turkey's *caudillo*, in Turkish *Milli Şef*, 'National Leader'. Anderson notes that during the Second World War 'İnönü had steered his country in much the way Franco had done Spain, tempering political affinity and passive assistance to the Nazi regime with a prudent *attentisme* allowing for better relations with the West once it looked as if Germany would be defeated.'[17] In the mid 1940s İnönü's regime purged left-wing academics from the universities and dispatched them into exile. They were not allowed to return to Turkey for decades. As mentioned earlier, in 1948, under İnönü's rule, the left-wing author Sabahattin Ali was brutally murdered by the Turkish secret service.

That a former right-wing *caudillo* would two decades later end up 'left of centre' is stunning, but it was a political manoeuvre dictated by tactical considerations, just as İnönü's earlier conversion to democracy had been. What İnönü tried to do was stave off what he saw as the threat of the rising radical left. Above all, he feared that the CHP was going to lose its position to the socialist TİP. His 'vision' of the left of centre was restricted to neutralizing the radical left; it had nothing in common with the radicalism of Ecevit. For a few years though, İnönü allowed the party's left wing to set the ideological tone, but the marriage of convenience between the old authoritarian and the young leftists of the CHP was soon to break up. When the right-wing coup took place in 1971, Ecevit took a strong stand against the military, correctly pointing out that the coup was a reaction to the rise of the left, and claiming that the coup makers wanted to crush his centre-left movement. In a sense, that was also correct. By 1971, İnönü had come to think that Ecevit had moved the party far too much to the left, and he saw the coup as an opportunity to settle accounts. İnönü endorsed the coup that the party secretary had condemned, in a blatant attempt to undermine Ecevit's position. Ecevit, though, stood his ground. He responded by challenging İnönü for the leadership of the party, and unseated him at the party congress in 1972. The left wing of the party was now in full command of the CHP.

But what exactly was it proposing to do? The smaller groupings on the radical left were annoyed to see the masses seduced by the charisma of Ecevit and pass them by; their reaction was to accuse Ecevit of imposture. He was not a true leftist, the radical leftists claimed. But when the right-wing violence escalated in the mid 1970s, the left united behind Ecevit. All leftist parties and organizations met up when Ecevit invited them to join him in a united, antifascist rally in Taksim Square in 1976, and all the different strands of the left backed the CHP in the general election in 1977. But of course, Ecevit was not a Marxist revolutionary. He was a social democratic reformist. He did however go a long way in challenging capitalist power. It was definitely not empty rhetoric when he said that 'This system must change!', as one of his books was titled. Indeed, this was Ecevit's signal rallying call; it electrified the crowds unlike any other political slogan had ever done before in Turkey. Ecevit promised an 'end to exploitation', land reform, workers' rights and income equality. It was no small change that he held out. He called it a 'people's revolution'. If it had not been aborted – we will see how that happened in the next chapter – it would certainly have revolutionized Turkish society.

The CHP's new economic programme stated that the private sector was no longer going to be allowed to dominate the economy; mines were to be nationalized and foreign capital regulated, with foreign companies prevented from transferring their profits out of Turkey. This, of course, was before the era of neoliberal globalization, when social democrats could still imagine challenging the power of capital. Yet this was not state socialism; it was not a version of leftism that would only end up empowering a parasitic bureaucracy. Ecevit was not the typical Third World socialist for whom socialism equalled state dominance of the economy; his economic vision was democratic, and it set him apart from the Kemalist left that admired the state 'socialism' of the Ba'ath party dictatorships in neighbouring Iraq and Syria. As I described earlier, the faction within the military that was drawn to this kind of Ba'ath-inspired state socialism, and which had been about to stage a coup, had been purged after the right-wing counter-coup in 1971. Ecevit's aim was to provide the people with a say over the economy; he challenged the state-private sector duality and introduced the idea of a 'people's sector' that was to co-exist with the state and private sectors. It was a kind of 'small-producer socialism'.

Ecevit made what in fact amounted to an ostentatious break with the legacy of the man who had founded the party he led: mobilizing Marxist terminology, he said that Atatürk's reforms had been all about superstructure and had not changed the conditions of the masses. In a widely read tract, *Atatürk ve devrimcilik* (Atatürk and being a revolutionary) – in which he first expounded on the notion of a 'secularism that is respectful of religion', a theme that he would cultivate throughout his political career – he asked rhetorically: 'the headgear reform was of course progressive, but what did it bring the people in terms of economic gains?'[18] The headgear had changed, but nothing else. Now, he promised, the 'base', the relations of production, was going to change. Ecevit tried to update Atatürk, or rather to reinterpret him, so that he would fit into his leftist vision: he held that to be a true follower of Atatürk meant working to improve the material conditions of the popular masses, not dressing up in tuxedos at officers' balls.

The peasants were going to be empowered through agricultural cooperatives and the industrial enterprises in which the cooperatives were to invest; as mentioned earlier, Ecevit was inspired by the example of the late-nineteenth-century Ottoman statesman and social and democratic reformer Mithat Pasha, who had organized an early version of what Ecevit named 'village-cities'; the idea was that local agricultural resources would be channelled to and jointly finance cooperatively owned craft and small-scale industrial production. A few such village-city initiatives were successfully launched when Ecevit became prime minister. The industrial workers, meanwhile, were to take part in the decision making of their companies – and step in as owners of the companies through trade union funds. Ecevit called it 'industrial democracy'. The idea was of Swedish social democratic origin: in 1976, Sweden's ruling social democrats passed a law that gave workers a say over the decision making of the companies that employed them. During the same period, the Swedish Trade Union Organization (LO) began to push for employee ownership of private companies; according to the plan, a part of the companies' profits was to be transferred to trade union funds. The unions would then use the funds to purchase shares in the companies. The idea met with strong opposition from the liberal and conservative parties and from capitalist circles in Sweden; even the Social Democratic Party was less than enthusiastic about what the bourgeois opposition dubbed 'employee socialism'. Ecevit, though, adopted the Swedish idea as part of his vision of an 'industrial democracy'.

During the 1970s, through the Socialist International that the CHP had joined, Ecevit developed a close relation in particular with Olof Palme, the leader of the Swedish social democrats. Palme was a fellow 'aristocratic radical', one of those leaders who had come to embody the progressive hope around the Western world during the late 1960s. Ecevit, who as we saw, first took his socialist inspiration from the British Labour Party, came to view Scandinavian socialism as a particularly promising alternative to emulate; the 1970s were indeed a time when the 'Swedish model' stood at its zenith. And as a beleaguered prime minister in the late 1970s, Ecevit would turn to the Scandinavian countries for financial aid. Yet even though many of his policy ideas were of Swedish social democratic origin, Ecevit chose not to label himself social democrat; instead, he used the term democratic left. It was a conscious choice that reflected his desire to emphasize that his ideas, their affinity with European social democratic thinking notwithstanding, were nonetheless ultimately anchored in the local culture of Turkey. He wanted to make a distinction between the Turkish left and a European social democracy that had once sprung from Marxism. That may seem rather curious, given both the reformist character of European social democracy, and the fact that much of Ecevit's own discourse in fact bore witness to the influence of Marxism. But he feared that he would be even more vulnerable to attacks from the right if he used a definition that, however distantly, could be linked to Marxism by the right-wing demagogues. 'Democratic left' was also a definition devised to demarcate his position from Soviet socialism.

Ecevit held that the culture of Turkey was informed by a historical legacy that made its people, so to speak, naturally predisposed to support the left; the left only had to avoid repelling the people with foreign, provocative associations, take care to speak its language, and respect its cultural and religious values. He insisted that there were 'seriously leftist' people among those who attended the mosque, but that these pious leftists had nowhere else to turn than to the right-wing parties because they were used to being cold-shouldered by the progressives. Indeed, the success of the CHP in the historic election of 1977 bore him out. The pious reciprocated when the left embraced them: 42 per cent of those who voted for the CHP were Muslims who followed the religious obligation to pray regularly. The CHP emerged as the winning party in the most conservative provinces in central Anatolia, including, sensationally, in Konya which was, and still is, a bastion of religious conservatism. Legitimating a leftist discourse with religious references had paid off handsomely; it had touched a chord among the pious peasantry when they heard Ecevit intone that 'The religion of Islam says that the land belongs to its tiller, and so does the CHP.'

Yet this was not cheap electoral tactic, or an act of imposture, as when the right-wing parties pretended to be on the side of the people when in fact they represented the interests of the powerful. Ecevit sincerely believed that the popular and religious culture of Anatolia was not only compatible but in harmony with leftist ideals. He extolled what was dubbed 'Anatolian humanism'. Other Turkish leftist intellectuals at

the time – the late 1960s and the 1970s – were also turning
to history to ground leftist politics in the indigenous culture.
Tolerance, democracy, progress, equality and solidarity were
held to be historically anchored in the depths of Anatolian
popular culture. Indeed, the syncretistic folk religion of
Anatolia was by definition open-minded. Ecevit pointed out
that, from the sixteenth century onwards, the orthodox state
Islam of the Ottomans had been resisted at the popular level,
and that the people of Anatolia had shaped their lives and
what religion meant to them independently of the central
administration.

The Ottoman system offered a curious combination of
freedom with centralized political control; as described in
Chapter 3, the Ottoman state prevented the emergence of a
class of landlords in Anatolia and ensured the survival of the
small peasantry there. Ottoman-ruled Anatolian society had
therefore been spared sharp class divisions, unlike what was
the case in medieval feudal Europe. Ecevit argued that this
had bequeathed a legacy of egalitarianism. The development
of a capitalist economy from the nineteenth century onward
introduced a new class dynamic, but it was nonetheless
reasonable to assume that the historical *longue durée* continued
to resonate in the present, and that deeply embedded egalitarian ideals would have survived in the societal subconscious of
Anatolia, providing the left with a 'naturally' receptive terrain.

Imagined or real, the concept of 'Anatolian humanism' was
useful in offering a framework for the reconciliation of the left
and the pious masses, of modernity and traditional culture. The
notion of an Anatolian-humanist left was sufficiently anchored
in the reality of popular, religious culture to not come across
as contrived. It did not require too much creative imagination

to reconcile leftist ideals and popular, syncretistic religiosity. Reconciling ethnic differences, however, is a different matter; there is no equivalent, living, Anatolian-humanist heritage to which to appeal in this regard. Of course, Turks, Kurds, Armenians, Greeks and others had co-existed and intermixed for ten centuries; indeed, the other ethno-cultural groups had been mixing since time immemorial, before the Turkic tribes arrived in the tenth century. There was a common Anatolian culture, with its shared mores, traditions and tastes. Armenian, Turkish and Kurdish folk music, for instance, sounds the same. But this culture was destroyed when rival ethnic nationalisms tore apart the social fabric of Anatolia; since the end of the nineteenth century, relations between the ethnic groups in Anatolia have been defined by anything but tolerance and humanism. In Chapter 3 I described how religion and ethnicity conjugated with capitalist dynamics to turn Anatolia into a killing field at the beginning of the twentieth century. And I have previously noted that Atatürk crushed two major Kurdish uprisings, in 1925 and in 1937-8. The Kurdish regions remained pacified until the late 1960s, when a new radical Kurdish nationalism rose. It would take more than an abstract notion of 'Anatolian humanism' to accommodate this new nationalism. Yet Ecevit took an idealistic view of Anatolia as a common home for its different ethnic groups. In 'The Ageless Woman of Pülümür', the poet Ecevit offered a beautiful homage to his country's heritage of cultural and ethnic heterogeneity:

I met her in a mountain village of Pülümür
I asked her age she smiled as a secret
Some said eighty some said hundred

I turned to her she smiled as a secret
She held a sceptre for a stick
She wore the velvet cloak
Of a faded kingdom
She was a Hittite she was a Seljuk
She was an Armenian she was a Kurd
A Turk
I asked her age she smiled as a secret
Graciously she took me by the arm
Dragging her cloak in the dusty village road
She took me to the single room palace
Of her village hut
I lost with her the sense of time
I reached with her the times lost
In the earthen-floored palace of exalted poverty
I was crowned with the grace of belonging to Turkey

Ecevit had passed through Pülümür, a small impoverished town in eastern Anatolia, when on a campaign tour in 1969. With 'The Ageless Woman of Pülümür', which is perhaps his most memorable poem, this forgotten town has earned a place in the Turkish literary canon. The poem is not only a beautiful ode to ethnic and cultural pluralism – it is also a brave work: it was written at a time when the mere mention of the word 'Kurd' was a subversive act. And its message – that what has made Turkey today are all those peoples, from the Hittites three millennia ago to the Armenians, Kurds and Turks who later populated and mixed in Anatolia – is an affront to right-wing Turkish nationalism that refuses to recognize anything but the Central Asian Turkic roots and Islam as the foundations of Turkey.

The nationalist Turkish military saw Ecevit as dangerous because he insisted that the challenge posed by Kurdish nationalism had to be met peacefully. Yet neither did he please the radical Kurdish left, which held him to be 'anti-Kurdish'. Hopelessly, Ecevit tried to find a middle way between Turkish and Kurdish nationalism: on the one hand he did his best – but failed – to check the military, and on the other he vainly argued that radical Kurdish nationalism would be neutralized if only social and economic measures were taken. The Kurdish areas in the south-east of Turkey were the poorest in the country, and Ecevit believed that underdevelopment was the cause of the radicalization. That was indeed partly true: the new leftist Kurdish nationalism was in equal measure an anti-feudal uprising – against the hold of the local, Kurdish feudal tribal leaders who were the beneficiaries of an archaic system that kept the masses in poverty – and a revolt against the oppressive Turkish state. Yet for the Kurdish radicals, the argument that social and economic development was the solution was a provocation, an affront, because it withheld the recognition of the Kurds as a separate people, which was what they craved above all. This was why, for them, Ecevit came across as an 'enemy of the Kurds'.

Ecevit was bound to fail as both sides – the Turkish nationalist military and the Kurdish nationalists – became more strident. In 1978, the Kurdistan Workers' Party (PKK) was founded. The PKK declared itself Marxist-Leninist, a stance that it downplayed after the dissolution of the Soviet Union. When the right-wing military took power in 1980, the prison in Diyarbakır, the main Kurdish city in Turkey, became infamous as one of the worst torture centres in the Turkish right's gulag. The military's barbarism fuelled a reaction: in

1984, the PKK started a rebellion against the Turkish state that has been ongoing intermittently ever since. At least 40,000 – mostly Kurdish militants – have lost their lives in the war, and millions of Kurdish citizens have suffered its consequences in one way or another. In the latest wave of violence, in 2015, the Turkish army laid several Kurdish cities in the south-east of the country to rubble when it dislodged the PKK militants, killing an unknown number of civilians in the process. The onslaught of the Turkish army in civilian population centres was condemned in a report by the United Nations.

It was not coincidental that the new Kurdish nationalism that gave rise to the PKK arose at the same time as the left did in the 1960s and 1970s; this was nationalism with a strong leftist accent. But it was religious conservatism that had, and still has, the strongest hold over the Kurds. Most Kurds identify themselves as Sunni Muslims first, and only thereafter by their ethnic identity. In every general election since 1950 – except in the election of June 2015 – the vast majority of Turkish Kurds have voted for the leading Turkish conservative party. The Kurdish vote has been crucial for keeping Erdoğan and his conservative party in power. Even though in the 1977 general election Ecevit succeeded in winning over the pious Turkish peasants and workers, he failed to make any inroads whatsoever among the Kurdish rural population; he simply stood too far to the left for the more religiously conservative Kurdish peasants. But neither could he satisfy the radicals.

Four decades later, it looked as if the promise of an Anatolian left stood a chance of being revived: that promise was embodied by Selahattin Demirtaş, co-chairman of the pro-Kurdish and officially democratic socialist Peoples' Democratic Party (HDP). A lawyer with a fine sense of humour, charm and charisma, Demirtaş was dubbed the 'Kurdish Kennedy'. HDP is secular and leftist, a combination that has otherwise always repelled the conservative Kurdish majority. Yet Demirtaş succeeded in winning over the religiously conservative Kurds, just as Ecevit had once succeeded in swaying the pious Turkish masses. And Demirtaş also demonstrated that he could reach across the ethnic divide and establish a rapport with leftist Turks. In the general election of June 2015, seven out of ten Kurdish votes went to the HDP. It was the first time ever that a majority of Kurds had rallied to a secular leftist party. And the HDP received votes from Turkish leftists as well. There were admittedly special circumstances that accounted for this success: Erdoğan had alienated the conservative Kurds with his Turkish nationalism and hostility toward them, while the Turkish leftist support was primarily, if not only, tactically motivated – a strong HDP representation would ensure that the parliamentary clout of Erdoğan's AKP was circumscribed. Indeed, the 13 per cent of the vote received by the HDP deprived the ruling AKP of its majority in parliament. Just like Ecevit in the 1970s, Demirtaş had become a threat to the system, to the hegemony of the right. In October 2016, Demirtaş and the leading cadres of the HDP, including members of parliament and mayors of the main Kurdish cities, were arrested, accused of 'terrorism'.

Ecevit's democratic leftist challenge to the system had come close to succeeding. But the vengeance of the right was about to be unleashed.

CHAPTER SIX

Vengeance of the Right

Years later, Bülent Ecevit recalled that it had been a close call. As his campaign bus made its way into the small town of Gerede in the Bolu province in north-west Anatolia, where he was scheduled to hold an election rally, rocks were hurled at it from the surrounding cliffs. The narrow passage through the mountains that led into Gerede made a perfect site for an ambush, but Ecevit and his party continued unharmed into the town. The date was 23 June 1975. A crowd of supporters had gathered to listen to *Karaoğlan*, the 'Black boy', as peasants and workers across Turkey had taken to calling Ecevit affectionately, because of his dark hair and features and his characteristic moustache that lent him a folksy air. It was a hypocorism signalling that the people had adopted him, the intellectual with his elite background, as one of their own. Huge crowds gathered everywhere Ecevit went, and a social democratic victory in the approaching election to the senate, the upper house of the Turkish parliament, beckoned.

But for this reason, there were also others, armed right-wing thugs, waiting for Ecevit. The 'greeting party' that had laid ambush to him had failed to stop him from entering the town, but he was not yet out of the woods, far from it. The worst was still to come. Other would-be assassins had taken up positions on balconies and roofs around the square where he was due to speak, while others had mixed with the crowd. They belonged to the Grey Wolves,[1] the armed militia of the fascist Nationalist Action Party (MHP), and to the youth organization of the Islamist National Salvation Party (MSP). The fascists and the Islamists had just formed an anti-democratic Nationalist Front government together with the main conservative party, the Justice Party of Prime Minister Süleyman Demirel. The Nationalist Front government was formed with a single political objective in mind: to crush the left. It went for the kill immediately after assuming power.

When Ecevit climbed on the roof of his campaign bus, which was fitted with a platform, to address the crowd, he was first met by another round of stones; soon, shots were fired at him from the surrounding balconies and roofs. At the same time, the right-wing thugs went on a rampage across the town, attacking leftist supporters and setting fire to their houses and properties. The police stood by passively as the stones were hurled at Ecevit; when the gunfire erupted, the police dispersed and promptly left the main square. Ecevit was left defenceless. One thing was clear: he was not supposed to leave Gerede alive. It was also evident that the assault against him and his supporters was carefully planned and coordinated, and that the police were in collusion with the fascist and Islamist thugs. Indeed, this was a pattern that was to be repeated over and over again during the remainder of the 1970s: not only could the fascist assassins act with impunity, they were also abetted by the police and the military.

It was obvious that the attempt to assassinate Ecevit enjoyed high-level political endorsement. Otherwise, the forces of order would not have acted as they did, or rather neglected to act. After Gerede, bodyguards would encircle Ecevit – and always with their guns drawn – whenever he addressed the crowds, but his party had apparently been unsuspecting on the day that the first, though not the last, attempt on his life was made. Ecevit was saved only because one of the accompanying CHP parliamentarians on his campaign bus, a medical doctor, had had the foresight to bring along a gun and was courageous enough to stand in as his personal bodyguard. He led Ecevit off the bus, gave him cover and managed to convey him to the relative safety of the local governor's office.

The formation of the Nationalist Front government had flung the doors of the Turkish state wide open for fascist assassins. The Grey Wolves were allowed to take control of all of the most critical ministries: the interior, justice and education ministries. By 1975, the fascists had started to carry out assassinations of university teachers and students; the universities were targeted because they had become strongholds of the left, like in so many other countries around the world at the time. When the fascists were given control of the ministry of education, violence against left-leaning teachers and students spread through the whole school system. With fascist entrenchment in the interior and justice ministries any semblance of the rule of law disappeared; now, fascist violence reigned supreme. Fascists were promoted in the police force, and the Grey Wolves had a carte blanche to execute leftists at will, without having to worry about any obstruction from the law enforcement agencies. The chief prosecutor in Ankara, though, refused to yield; he heroically tried to uphold the law and prosecute the fascist killers – and he paid for it with his life. Doğan Öz was assassinated on 24 March 1978.

It was obvious to everyone that the governing Nationalist Front was fomenting the fascist violence; indeed, the prime minister, the conservative leader Demirel, in effect condoned it. He and other mainstream bourgeois politicians held the Grey Wolves to be nationalist 'idealists' who were doing nothing but performing a patriotic duty, defending the state against the threat of 'communist subversion'. 'You are never going to make me say that the nationalist youth are assassins', Demirel said.[2] The fascist violence escalated under government protection. Students and left-wing intellectuals were the main targets; several of Turkey's finest academics and intellectuals were assassinated. As I pointed out in Chapter 1, a pattern of massacres was set: on 1 May 1977, unidentified snipers opened fire on the Labour Day rally at Taksim Square in Istanbul, killing at least 40. On 16 March 1978, seven students were killed when a bomb was detonated at the University of Istanbul. Turkey's main trade union organization, the Revolutionary Trade Union Confederation (DİSK) responded to those killings by calling on workers to stop work for an hour as a 'warning to fascism'. The call was heeded by 600,000 workers, who staged a nationwide protest against the violence. But the fascists were undeterred. On 8 October 1978, the Grey Wolves carried out one of their most hideous acts: they stormed a house in Ankara where seven university students, all members of the socialist Labour Party of Turkey, were living and brutally killed all of them.

At the beginning of 1978, Ecevit unexpectedly managed to unseat the Nationalist Front government. But it was to prove to be a Pyrrhic victory. Social democracy acceded to power only in name, and at the worst possible time, when it stood little chance of accomplishing anything. In fact, Ecevit had cobbled together an unwieldy coalition government, with the participation of a group of defectors from the conservative party. The social democrats had carried the general election of June 1977, but the result had left them 13 seats short of a parliamentary majority, and the Nationalist Front could return to power.

Ecevit was deeply worried about how the Nationalist Front government had allowed the fascist Grey Wolves to become entrenched in the state machinery. In the fall of 1977, he received information that the fascists were also establishing close contacts with the military. He began to fear that preparations were underway to stage a fascist coup. One can assume that many in the officers' corps were indeed fascist-leaning at this time, but it is nonetheless important to make a distinction between fascism and 'ordinary' right-wing authoritarianism: traditionally, the Turkish military has been strongly nationalist and anti-leftist, so overall it is fair to describe it as right-wing authoritarian, even though, as we saw earlier, there was a significant left-wing current in the military during the 1960s. Fascism flourished in the ranks of the military during the Second World War, when the example of the Nazis inspired ideas of establishing a pan-Turkic empire from Anatolia to Central Asia. But after the defeat of the Nazis, the Turkish high command took severe measures to check the fascists, and the leading pro-Nazi in the army, Alparslan Türkeş, was briefly interned.

A decade later, as we saw earlier, Colonel Türkeş was the leading force behind Turkey's first coup, in 1960, but he was subsequently purged from the junta that had taken power when he resisted the return to civilian democratic rule. He later went on to form the fascist Nationalist Action Party. He fancied himself *Başbuğ*, the Turkish equivalent of *Führer*. In 1975, the would-be *Führer* of Turkey entered the government as deputy prime minister in the Nationalist Front. With the benediction of the conservative prime minister, he set about populating the state apparatus with his fascist killers.

Figure 6   Mimicking Hitler: Alparslan Türkeş, the Turkish fascist leader. The militia of his party, the 'Grey Wolves', killed thousands of leftists between 1975 and 1980.

The dynamics of the relationship between the bourgeois parties and the fascists were more or less the same as the dynamics of the military-fascist relation: the conservatives and the military had no compunction in soliciting the services of the fascists – or turning a blind eye to their deadly deeds – in order to stamp out the class enemies of the bourgeoisie, but they did not intend to relinquish the state permanently to the fascists. Indeed, when a right-wing – neoliberal and nationalist to be precise – military dictatorship was imposed in 1980, many of the Grey Wolves who had prepared the ground for it were also, to their own great astonishment, dispatched to prison. Unlike the innocent leftists, the fascist assassins were never subjected to torture, nor were any of them beaten to death or executed as hundreds of leftists were, but they were still enraged and humiliated at being rewarded with a prison stint, however brief, for the services they had performed. The fascist *Başbuğ* put it rather succinctly when he said, 'We are in prison, but our ideas are in power.'

In the fall of 1977, Ecevit feared that a different version of a fascist takeover was imminent. He was receiving indications that plans for a coup were being hatched, but he also worried that, if the Nationalist Front remained in power, the fascists could ultimately take full control of the government without having to stage a coup. It was therefore imperative to bring down the Front government, at any cost and as soon as possible. To save Turkey from fascism, Ecevit felt compelled to strike an unseemly bargain with a group of conservative dissenters: he persuaded 11 of the conservative party's members of parliament to defect from their party and support him as prime minister; in return, they were all rewarded with seats in the government he was then able to form. Some of his party colleagues questioned both the ethics and the political wisdom of ascending to government in this unbecoming way, while others on the contrary urged him to strike a bargain, and if necessary even offer the conservative parliamentarians big sums of money.

Ecevit's makeshift government would last from January 1978 until November 1979, but it never wielded any power over the state machinery nor did it have any influence over the course of events. Ecevit was powerless to check the fascist violence, let alone implement any of his ambitious social and economic reforms. He became a tragic figure: besieged by the bourgeoisie, he would ultimately also forfeit the support of his base, the workers and peasants, who, disgusted with his lack-lustre performance, would cast their votes for the right at the first opportunity. Those in the CHP who had been critical of the bargain with the conservative defectors were proven right in their warnings: the lack of internal cohesion paralyzed the government. An ideological gulf separated the social democratic CHP and the conservatives Ecevit had rewarded with ministerial portfolios, but it was always Ecevit who had to concede, as when the minister of industry, a conservative, vetoed his Swedish-inspired attempt to introduce industrial democracy. The conservatives had this oversized influence because they held the keys to the government's survival. The conservative industry minister claimed that giving the workers a decision-making role in their companies would amount to 'communism'. Indeed, the perception of Ecevit as a crypto-communist was widespread in business circles and, damningly for him, in the military.

The military high command viewed the social democratic prime minister with mistrust, and increasingly with open hostility. To start with, the military was weary of Ecevit's resistance to their plans to use violence against the Kurds. There had in fact as yet been no Kurdish uprising, but signs of assertiveness were accumulating and that was enough to irk the military: slogans such as 'Freedom to the Kurds' on walls, and the display of Kurdish placards during the Labour Day celebrations in Kurdish cities in the south-east in 1978, set off alarm bells in the military headquarters in Ankara. The use of Kurdish was officially banned, and yet local Kurdish CHP parliamentarians had taken part in the 1 May celebrations without objecting to the display of the placards in Kurdish, and Ecevit had not held them to account for having done so. And as if that was not enough, he had had the impertinence to argue against the generals when they called for the use of force to pacify the Kurdish regions. In the eyes of the military, the prime minister was a 'traitor', an epithet the officers started to use openly when referring to him.

When, shortly after becoming prime minister, Ecevit chose to make his first foreign trip to Yugoslavia, suspicions were aroused among the officers' corps that he was going to try to introduce some version of the Yugoslav system – a socialist, federated state in which the composing nations enjoyed a degree of autonomy. The military also began to fear that Ecevit would call Turkey's adherence to NATO into question, and that he entertained plans to edge the country toward a non-aligned position. The latter suspicions were not entirely unfounded. Ecevit was trying his hand at a kind of *ostpolitik,* or rather a *nordpolitik*: a little bit like the former social democratic chancellor of West Germany, Willy Brandt, who had opened relations with East Germany and Poland a few years earlier, Ecevit wanted to explore the possibilities of forging new relationships with non-aligned Yugoslavia, as well as with Romania, a country pursuing what seemed to be a more independent foreign policy within the Warsaw Pact, but also with the Scandinavian countries, in particular neutral Sweden, where, however, his social democrat friends had recently lost power after half a century in government. Ecevit did not think that Turkey could leave NATO, but he did hope, vainly as it turned out, that a 'northern' reorientation would make Turkey less dependent on the United States.

The American Intervention

Turkey's geography has been a curse for its democracy, as the course of events in the second half of the 1970s tragically demonstrated. Turkey was the easternmost garrison of NATO in the Cold War, which made it indispensable for the United States. Its location also made the country a place where the dynamics of the Cold War 'naturally' militated against the left and democracy: a turn to the left in such a geopolitically sensitive place was bound to incite American countermeasures. In the late 1940s, the right-wing regime in Turkey had actively sought to be accepted into the Western alliance since it was obsessed with a largely imaginary threat from the Soviet Union, but NATO membership had in fact made Turkey more, not less vulnerable. In 1960, an American U2 high-altitude reconnaissance plane that had taken off from a US airbase in Turkey was shot down over the Soviet Union, causing a major crisis at a time of rising tensions, which were to culminate with the Cuban missile crisis in 1962. Turkey became another pawn in the superpower game: in return for the dismantlement of the Soviet missiles in Cuba, President John F. Kennedy made a secret pledge to the Soviet leader Nikita Khrushchev that the United States would withdraw the nuclear missiles it had stationed in Turkey. By the end of the 1970s, after the fall of the Shah in Iran, Turkey's strategic value for the United States as a forward base on the border with the Soviet Union increased, which was to have dire consequences for its democracy and for the left.

The loss of Iran deprived Washington of a Middle Eastern client state and of a critical geopolitical asset. Iran bordered the Muslim Soviet republics of Azerbaijan in the Caucasus and Turkmenistan in Central Asia; it was both a barrier to what the American hawks had persuaded themselves the Soviets were preparing for – a southward expansion to grab oilfields in the Middle East – and a staging area for covert US actions to destabilize the Muslim regions of the Soviet Union. After the Shah left Iran in January 1979, America came to expect more cooperation from Turkey as compensation, but the social democratic Turkish leader was less than forthcoming. Ecevit was not the kind of militantly anti-communist, anti-Soviet leader the Americans wished for, on the contrary. He was in no way pro-Soviet, but like other leading European social democratic leaders – Willy Brandt, Olof Palme and the Austrian chancellor Bruno Kreisky – he wanted to de-escalate the Cold War and believed in the concept of common security for the Western and Eastern blocs. When he visited Washington, Ecevit displeased his host, President Jimmy Carter, by saying that Turkey was threatened not by the Soviet Union, but by Greece, a country with which war had indeed been close in 1974. Back then, the right-wing military junta that ruled Greece had tried to annex Cyprus, to which Ecevit – leading his first government, a short-lived coalition – had responded by ordering an invasion of the island in order to prevent a Greek takeover. Ecevit refused to play by the American book. The CIA assessed him as a 'neutral or moderately anti-Western' leader,[3] and the US administration was growing increasingly apprehensive about a Turkish leader whom it manifestly could not control.

Things came to a head a few months after the CIA made their assessment, in a meeting on 7 May 1979 between Ecevit and Warren Christopher, deputy secretary of state in the Carter administration. Christopher unexpectedly arrived in Ankara on an urgent mission: to get the Turks to acquiesce to a resumption of U2 flights over the Soviet Union that had been discontinued after the downing of the plane in 1960. Christopher showed up in Ankara three days before the United States and the Soviet Union were due to sign the SALT 2 agreement on the limitation of nuclear warheads. As Christopher explained to Ecevit, the US administration was concerned about how it was going to monitor whether the Soviets were complying with the agreement. The American emissary told the Turkish prime minister that the situation had become more difficult after the closure of the US installations in Iran, that its satellites did not offer a clear enough view, and that therefore the United States needed to resume the U_2 spy flights from Turkey. When he asked Ecevit to give his permission, his host stiffened. Ecevit reminded Christopher about a conversation he had had with his boss, the secretary of state Cyrus Vance, when the latter had visited Ankara a year earlier. Ecevit had asked Vance to get the Soviets to acquiesce to the presence of the US monitoring facilities in Turkey as part of the then ongoing negotiations to reach the SALT 2 agreement. He told Christopher that he had pointed out to Vance that the Soviets were extremely sensitive about these secret installations and that he feared that they might make Turkey 'pay for them' by stirring up unrest and terrorism. Ecevit inquired if the Americans had raised the issue of these installations during the SALT 2 negotiations as he had asked them to do. No, they had not, Christopher replied. 'Well then, reach an agreement with them', Ecevit told him. He was certainly not going to acquiesce to any secret U_2 flights, and did not mince his words: 'You cannot undertake such secret missions from here. That would provoke the Soviet Union',[4] he said. His guest was outraged, threatening that the economic assistance Turkey expected from the United States might be endangered.

Ironically, while Washington and the Turkish military suspected that Ecevit was a crypto-communist who was, at best, soft on the Soviets and at worst pro-Soviet, he was in fact cold-shouldered by Moscow. If Ecevit had had any illusions about the Soviets they were dissipated when he visited Moscow in June 1978. Turkey's economy was in free fall; the country's foreign currency reserves were depleted, which had led to energy shortages that further paralyzed the economy since the country could not pay for oil imports. Maybe the Soviet Union could help out, the Turkish government wondered. Ecevit's deputy prime minister pleaded with the Soviets: he asked them to dispatch just one oil tanker, and to accept credit payment. The Soviets were anything but forthcoming; they would only accept payment in cash, in US dollars. They had no incentive to help the cause of social democracy in Turkey. The Soviets cared little about the democratic left Ecevit represented in the first place, and they knew that Turkey would anyway always remain in the American camp. The borders that separated the two enemy blocs in the Cold War were carved in stone.

The May 1979 meeting between Ecevit and Christopher was the breaking point for the United States. Ecevit had to go, Washington concluded. The news that filtered out from the foreign policy and security establishment in Washington starting in May 1979 suggested that a consensus had been reached in policy circles that Ecevit could not, or rather should not, govern Turkey. Only the military, the reasoning went, could 'restore stability' in Turkey. It may have been the post-Watergate era, but the Carter administration had no compunction in following in the footsteps of the Nixon administration in dealing with annoyingly leftist foreign leaders. Henry Kissinger, Nixon's secretary of state, had been the mastermind behind the coup in Chile against the socialist president Salvador Allende in 1973. Zbigniew Brzezinski, the national security advisor to Jimmy Carter, now played a somewhat similar role in the case of Turkey and its social democratic leader: he more or less openly encouraged the Turkish military to get rid of Ecevit, and to cancel democracy in the name of 'stability'.

Brzezinski was the archetypal Cold Warrior. He was the architect of the secret American scheme to destabilize and ultimately bring down the Soviet Union by fomenting an Islamic insurgency against the communist regime that had seized power in Afghanistan in 1978. The plan was to lure the Soviets into Afghanistan and get them bogged down in their own Vietnam War. Moscow walked into the trap. Six months after President Carter had authorized the CIA to arm and train the Islamic fighters, the 'mujahedin', in Afghanistan, the Soviets, fearing that the insurgency would spread to its Muslim Central Asian republics that bordered Afghanistan, invaded the country. The American plan worked perfectly, but the United States had embarked on a path that was going to lead to the al-Qaeda terrorist attacks of 11 September 2001. It is useful to remember that jihadist terrorism, and Islamism in general, is ultimately a product of the Cold War strategies devised in Washington in the 1970s. Even so, the architect of the policy, Brzezinski, had no regrets: 'What is more important in a world historical perspective – the Talibans or the fall of the Soviet Empire; a few frantic Islamists or the liberation of central Europe and the end of the Cold War?' he asked.[5]

Brzezinski was disgusted with Ecevit. He railed that Ecevit did not know what he was talking about, and that it was unheard of to ask for the permission of the enemy, as Ecevit had asked the United States to do, to maintain spy installations on Turkish soil. Addressing a group of Turkish businessmen who visited Washington in 1979, after the meeting with Ecevit, Brzezinski was blunt, telling his guests that 'Turkey will not get anywhere with that man.'[6] The intentions of the US administration could not have been made clearer, and one can assume that the Turkish businessmen were relieved to hear Brzezinski speak the way he did about a man who had vowed to change their country's capitalist system. We can also assume that the question of how 'stability' was going to be restored in Turkey was explored in the discussions that the chief of the Turkish general staff, General Kenan Evren, had with Brzezinski and other US officials when he spent two whole weeks in Washington in June 1979. Publicly, the American hosts expressed their worry that 'stability' eluded Turkey, but it is safe to assume that the discussions behind closed doors focused on what ought to be done to deal with the annoying fact that Turkey was led by a headstrong leftist. It may well have been on this occasion that Evren got the American green light for a coup, but Brzezinski had in any case already practically given a go-ahead for the overthrow of Ecevit.

Evren would officially assume full powers in the coup of September 1980, but the general staff had in fact already succeeded in bending Ecevit to its will. To all intents and purposes, it was no longer the government but the military that was in charge. Ecevit was left with no alternative but to yield what little power he had to the military when the Grey Wolves carried out a pogrom against left-leaning Alevis in December 1978. After the pogrom in the city of Kahraman-maraş, Ecevit had to acquiesce to the generals' demand that he declare martial law, which put the military in direct charge in 13 out of Turkey's 67 provinces, including in the capital Ankara and in Istanbul, the most populous city of the country.

Under martial law, democratic freedoms were suspended. The military takeover of Turkey had begun.

In Latin American Footsteps

On 21 December 1978, the Grey Wolves took control of the city of Kahramanmaraş in south-eastern Anatolia where the Alevis made up a significant part of the population, and went on a killing spree that lasted for almost a week. As I mentioned in the first chapter, the Alevis practice a heterodox, liberal version of Islam, and they have historically been oppressed and punished for their deviation from Islamic orthodoxy. The Alevis have also always belonged to the socially under-privileged, which has made them a natural constituency for the left in Turkey. The same dynamic once played out in Iraq and Lebanon, where the equally socially dispossessed Shiites, used to provide most of the cadres for the communist parties, before communism crumbled and was replaced with religious contestation movements.

Kahramanmaraş is a compound word, with 'kahraman', which means hero, added to the original name of the city, Maraş. It is supposed to evoke what is held to be a glorious past: according to official Turkish historiography, the city put up a heroic resistance to its French occupiers during the Anatolian war that followed the First World War, for which it was rewarded with the new name. In fact, much of the population of Maraş was Armenian, and the Armenians saw the French not as occupiers but as liberators. When the Turkish national forces defeated the French and drove them out of the city in 1920, they massacred thousands of Armenians, setting a historic precedent for what was to follow half a century later.

The pogrom against the Alevis in Kahramanmaraş went on between 21 December and 25 December. Unhindered by the military or the police, the Grey Wolves slaughtered Alevis and others who were known to be leftist sympathizers and set fire to their houses. The military was not only criminally passive: soldiers also actively abetted in the killings. People who sought the protection of the military were handed over to the Grey Wolves who promptly executed them. Ecevit dispatched his interior, justice and health ministers to Kahramanmaraş to assess the situation. But the government delegation was prevented from entering the city; the ministers were assaulted, and the health minister was nearly lynched by the fascists. Ecevit now instructed his interior minister, a former general, to seek out Alparslan Türkeş, the leader of the fascist MHP and of the Grey Wolves, and reason with him. It was a desperate and naive bid to get Türkeş to halt the killing spree. Under normal conditions, the fascist leader would have been arrested, and the military commanders and the chief of the national police held to account for their criminal negligence in maintaining order and protecting citizens. But these were anything but normal circumstances; democratic governance had been overrun by fascism and militarism. Presumably Ecevit hoped that Türkeş, a former colonel, would show some reverence for the interior minister because he was a former general. The fascist leader, though, was unmoved. He flatly told the social democrat interior minister that the 'Idealists [the official name of the fascist militia] are assisting the forces of order.'[7] He had thus no reason to call them back. The Grey Wolves were doing nothing wrong: they were helping to keep the country safe from socialist disorder. The fascist militia was indeed assisting the forces of order, as Türkeş said: it was doing the dirty work of the system. The Grey Wolves' mission was to create the conditions that would legitimize the imposition of martial law, and later a full military dictatorship, to ensure that 'stability' could be duly 'restored'. According to the official account, 111 people were killed and more than 1,000 wounded, while 552 houses and 289 workplaces were destroyed. In all likelihood, the number of casualties greatly exceeded the official account; they are estimated to have been several thousand. The dramatic proportions of the pogrom are underscored by the fact that it precipitated a wave of refugees from the city, with 80 per cent of the Alevi population leaving it.

The pogrom against the Alevis had three purposes: to inspire fear among the left and break its resolve, to undermine Ecevit's position and make him subservient to the military, and to provide the pretext for the imposition of martial law. The spirit of the left was not necessarily broken, although the mood was understandably gloomy. What really disabled the left was its failure to maintain a united front in face of the fascist and militarist onslaught; the campaign of right-wing violence succeeded in driving a wedge between Ecevit and the labour movement. The latter committed a grave mistake, and played into the hands of the right, when it abandoned Ecevit after 1 May 1979. The trade union confederation DİSK unjustly blamed Ecevit when the military used the authority of martial law to ban the 1 May celebrations. In Istanbul, the general who was now the de facto governor of the city also declared a curfew on 1 May. The workers who disobeyed the ruling and attempted to march toward the city's Taksim Square, where 1 May was traditionally celebrated, were arrested by the military. Ecevit protested, and asked the military to release them, but to no avail. His words no longer carried any weight whatsoever.

Shortly afterwards, the general representing Turkey at the NATO headquarters in Brussels proudly told the US general Alexander Haig, who commanded the NATO forces in Europe, that the military commander in Istanbul had broken up the workers' attempt to celebrate Labour Day, and that he was going to ignore the objections of the government and keep the workers detained. Haig, Ronald Reagan's future secretary of state, was duly impressed: 'Bravo! Now, that's what I call a commander. That's how you install stability', he exclaimed.[8]

The pogrom in Kahramanmaraş dealt a crushing blow to Ecevit. To all intents and purposes, it finished him off politically; first, because he had to cave in to the military and acquiesce to it taking control over most of the country; second, because he forfeited the support of the labour movement as a result. A month later, on 1 February 1979, Ecevit was dealt yet another blow when his leading supporter in the press, the editor in chief of the influential centre-left daily *Milliyet*, Abdi İpekçi, was assassinated. İpekçi had played an important role in disseminating social democratic ideas in Turkey since the 1960s, and he had given Ecevit precious media attention when he began his ascent to power. He had in a sense legitimized Ecevit's leftist ideas among the enlightened upper middle class in Istanbul to which he belonged. Those who commissioned the murder of İpekçi clearly intended to deprive Ecevit of his voice in the media and in bourgeois circles. İpekçi hailed from the *Dönme* community, Ottoman Jews settled in the city of Salonika, now Thessaloniki in Greece, who had converted to Islam in the seventeenth century and who have maintained their identity as a distinct group in Turkey since then. The literal meaning of the noun *dönme* is 'to have turned'. Abdi İpekçi's background is worth mentioning because it provides a historical context for the role that he played as a promoter of progressive ideas: *Dönmes* formed a significant part of the intellectual avant-garde in the late Ottoman Empire, and they were indeed the leading force behind the 1908 Young Turk revolution. *Dönmes* dominated among the cadres and the leadership of the Young Turk movement. Anti-Semitic Islamists have therefore taken the secularism of the Young Turks and of their successors, the Kemalists, as proof of a supposed Jewish conspiracy against Islam. As described in earlier chapters, the Young Turks degenerated into chauvinist-nationalists, but they were initially motivated by genuinely liberal and progressive ambitions. That was the tradition that İpekçi had upheld. He was 50 years old when he was killed.

Class and politics were inverted in the İpekçi assassination: while the victim was a progressive who belonged to the Istanbul bourgeoisie, his assassin, a fascist Grey Wolf, hailed from socially destitute conditions in rural Anatolia. But Mehmet Ali Ağca enjoyed high-level protection; he happened to be apprehended, which was highly unusual for fascist killers, but the military authorities who were now in charge – as martial law had been declared – acted to control the damage and prevented the social democrat interior minister from interfering in the case. The minister had asked the police to investigate who had commissioned the murder, but the military governor of Istanbul ruled that Ağca was not going to be interrogated in the matter. After six months in prison, the assassin was escorted to freedom; the soldiers who guarded him helped him out of the prison and accomplices in the police saw to it that Ağca could safely leave the country with his papers in order. In 1981, Ağca shot Pope John Paul II in Rome. It was never clarified why he had tried to kill the pope.

Ultimately, the fascists' killing campaign served specific material interests in society, those of big business; however, the businessmen and the industrialists had kept a low profile, waiting for the violence against the left to deliver the political results they anticipated. But in 1979, the business community issued what amounted to no less than a coup memorandum to the social democrat-led government. The Association of Turkish Industrialists and Businessmen (TÜSİAD) had been founded in 1971, representing the most powerful conglomerates in Turkey, with the explicit purpose of providing an ideological-political counter-platform to the powerful labour movement. In 1979, the association went on the political offensive with full-page advertisements in the press against the government, which was accused of ruining the country. Ecevit was furious: 'It is not the businessmen who decide who is going to govern this state; governments are not brought down by the memoranda of businessmen, it is the word of the people that rules in this country, not the word of those who exploit the people.' Ecevit also reacted to the fact that while left-wing trade union leaders were prosecuted for making political statements, business leaders got away with interfering in politics. 'How can that be?' he asked, adding: 'I am going to send them all to court.'[9] It was a desperate statement. Soon the people were to turn against Ecevit. In by-elections later that year, the democratic left crashed from the 42 per cent it had received two years earlier to under 30 per cent; the conservative party was the big winner, soaring to nearly 50 per cent.

Fascist death squads, the military, the United States and the institutions of international capital had laid siege on Ecevit. He had spent nearly two years as prime minister caught in their crossfire; he had been powerless to stem the fascist violence or to withstand the blackmail of the International Monetary Fund, which demanded austerity measures that hit the working class in return for acquiescing to loans to Turkey. Someone had to be blamed, and as is usually the case, whatever its actual responsibility, it was the government. The working class and the peasants defected to the right at the first opportunity, in the elections in October 1979. Ecevit resigned. The leader of the right, Demirel, returned as prime minister. But the victory of the right was not yet complete. Ecevit had been finished off, but the labour movement was still an obstacle to the implementation of the neoliberal economic policies the business community were calling for. It was in fact a schizophrenic situation, with little correlation between the working-class voting pattern and its trade union activism. The working class cast its vote overwhelmingly for the conservatives at the ballot box, but it remained defiantly militant in the workplace: the radically leftist DİSK counted 500,000 members, and the number of strikes increased rapidly, from a yearly average of 65 between 1973 and 1976, to an average of 190 strikes between 1977 and 1980.

On 24 January 1980, the conservative government launched a neoliberal revolution. The public sector was to be slashed and the forces of the market set free. The 'reform package' had been prescribed by the IMF and the World Bank, and it was inspired by the theories of the American neoliberal economist Milton Friedman that were now increasingly in vogue around the world. Friedman had recently advised the military junta in Chile. Turkey was soon to follow in Latin American footsteps, with a military junta implementing neoliberal policies. The conservative government announced a freeze on public investments and huge cuts in the public sector; it declared its fealty to the new economic dogma, according to which the sole mission of the government was to ensure fiscal discipline and to keep inflation in check. The programme had two straightforward strategic purposes: to open up Turkey to international capital, and to empower capital in relation to labour. The trade unions went on strike in protest, and the question now was how their resistance was to be neutralized. Ecevit made a prescient prediction: he pointed out that the new economic regime in fact required a new political regime. He identified the model that was introduced as a 'new step in the system of exploitation'. Turkey was going to be subjected to international capital, he said, with the rich becoming richer and the poor becoming poorer. The rich have indeed become richer, and the economic inequalities have grown, but it is also a fact that poverty has diminished during the last decades.

Turkish conservatives had always held up capitalist America as a model, and said that they wanted Turkey to become a 'little America', but Ecevit saw that things were headed in a different direction with the new economy that was being imposed: he remarked that Turkey 'is not going to become a Little America, but Latin America'. He correctly predicted that it was going to be impossible for the governing conservative party to push through the neoliberal model within the existing democratic framework, and intimated that the military was going to take over in order to effect the change. That was indeed what happened.

Martial law gave the military commanders extraordinary powers to uphold order and guarantee the security of citizens, yet the violence still continued unabated. On 22 July 1980, the founding leader of the Revolutionary Trade Union Confederation, DİSK, Kemal Türkler, was assassinated. But now, leftists were hitting back; two days earlier, members of a left-wing group had killed the former prime minister of the right-wing military regime between 1971 and 1973. The violence that the military had done nothing to stop provided it with the pretext to stage its coup. On 12 September 1980, the chief of the general staff, General Kenan Evren finally took over as head of state. The killing that had plagued the country since 1975, when the fascist Grey Wolves started assassinating left-wing intellectuals, teachers and students, ceased overnight. Everything that the right-wing parties had worked to accomplish since the mid 1960s – restricting or even suspending the democratic liberties that empowered the labour movement and the left – was now swiftly carried out by the military junta. All democratic and social rights were abolished. DİSK, the main trade union organization, was banned and its leadership was arrested. Five hundred thousand people, the vast majority of them leftist activists, were incarcerated; 55 people were executed, while several hundred died under torture. In a note to his party friends, penned at the military base where he had been confined, Bülent Ecevit wrote: 'We are entering a period that will be extremely difficult for the left in all its shades. We need to be prepared for the very long and arduous road that lies ahead of us.'[10] Ecevit probably did not realize just how long the road was going to be, and how arduous the task; four decades later, the left in Turkey is still yet to recover from the crushing blow of 12 September 1980.

In Washington, President Jimmy Carter was informed about the coup in Turkey by his national security staff, who told him that 'our boys have done it'. *Time* magazine honoured the Turkish coup maker Kenan Evren on its cover: it portrayed a jovial Evren, and the accompanying headline read 'Holding

Turkey Together'. The Turkish business community was relieved. The chairman of the employers' union said that 'now, it's our turn to laugh'. He claimed that all laws that had been enacted since the 1960s had favoured labour, and said that he now looked forward to an era when the employers' interests were going to govern. Religious conservatives as well could look forward to a shining future. The preacher Fethullah Gülen was one of these. Gülen was to play a most prominent role in Turkish politics in the following decades: his political-religious movement, later to be known as the Gülenists, was going to take over most of the state establishment and provide indispensable support to Erdoğan, until a power struggle broke apart their arrangement, as we will see in the following chapter. After the coup in 1980, Gülen, then still an obscure preacher, saluted the military and lauded it for having saved the country from communism. Years later, Gülen said that 'Evren pasha', the general who had staged the coup, had earned himself a place in paradise because he had made education in Sunni Islam mandatory throughout the school system.

The neoliberal restructuring of Turkey and the promotion of religious influence went hand in hand. The supposedly 'secularist' Turkish military bolstered Islam. As noted earlier, Evren told the people that it had to embrace its religion firmly, and boasted that he was a son of a mullah. Religious education was vastly expanded and the military promoted a new 'Turkish-Islamic synthesis', a mishmash of Turkish nationalism and Islam which, as we saw in Chapter 4, right-wing intellectuals had concocted in the 1970s. But the junta did not really invent anything new. In Chapter 4, I described how in the 1940s the rulers of Turkey had already started using religion to 'inoculate' the population against leftist temptations. The junta in the 1980s simply applied nationalist-religious indoctrination much more systematically. The indoctrination of the young after 1980 has been achieved not only with the expansion of religious education, but also by the suffocation of left-wing thought. The junta purged all left-wing teachers from the universities, which laid waste to an entire intellectual tradition that had been built up during the preceding decades. In a sense, it was a 'cultural revolution' similar to that undertaken by Atatürk. But where Atatürk had assaulted religion, General Evren took on the left. And the junta leader was more successful than Atatürk in severing the bonds to the past and to an intellectual tradition – although of course the roots of religious tradition went incomparably deeper than the leftist roots did.

A similar process had taken place in Egypt during the 1970s, when President Anwar Sadat had bolstered religion and Islamic movements in order to stamp out the influence of the left, which was strong particularly among the young and in the universities, as he set about liberalizing the economy. Sadat paid for this tactic with his life – he was assassinated by Islamic militants in 1981, having failed to control the demons he had let out of the bottle. But in Turkey, Islamic influence was going to serve the needs of the bourgeois order well, as we are about to see.

CHAPTER SEVEN

The Rise of the Islamists

'Long live Islam, Allah is great', they chanted. It was 16 February 1969. The US Sixth Fleet had just anchored in Istanbul. Left-wing university students had taken to the streets by the Bosporus, the waterway that separates the European and Asian sides of Istanbul – and of Turkey – to protest against the American warships that lay at anchor, when another crowd of students showed up to shout them down with Islamic slogans. Here was an early demonstration that the United States could count on Islamists as allies against the left. At the head of the conservative Islamic crowd shouting religious slogans was a man named İsmail Kahraman. He was the president of the National Turkish Student Association (MTTB), the leading youth organization of the Turkish right. Today, Kahraman is the speaker of the Turkish parliament and a prominent member of the Islamic conservative Justice and Development Party (AKP) led by Recep Tayyip Erdoğan, Turkey's president since 2014, and before that prime minister from 2003 to 2014. Erdoğan was not present among the right-wing counter-protesters when they confronted the leftists by the Bosporus, but he had joined the right's student association that same year, 1969. He had just turned 15.

Erdoğan's original political identity was that of a religiously devout Cold Warrior. Nicolas Cheviron and Jean-François Pérouse, the authors of a detailed biography of Erdoğan, remark that the MTTB became a veritable 'university' for him, the place where he received his ideological formation.[1] He quickly rose in the ranks of the association, and by the mid 1970s had become one of its 'pillars', his biographers note. It was a strongly conservative milieu, where the three dimensions of Turkish right-wing ideology – conservatism, pan-Turkic fascism and Islam – were closely nested. From its foundation in 1916, its symbol was that of pan-Turkic fascism, the grey wolf, but it was replaced with an open book, an implicit reference to the Quran, in 1975. 'The only force that can destroy communism is Islam' was one of its slogans; 'Fighting against communism is as beneficial as praying' went another. The MTTB mobilized students from religiously conservative and lower-middle-class backgrounds as foot soldiers in the battle against socialism. Erdoğan became a leading figure in the association at a time when the right, as we saw in the preceding chapter, was waging a violent class war against the left. He was born in 1954 in a working-class district in Istanbul. His father was employed by the company responsible for public transportation on the Bosporus,[2] and both he and Erdoğan's mother hailed from the province of Rize in the Black Sea region, close to the border with Georgia. Erdoğan's ethnic origins have been a matter of controversy; as noted in the preceding chapters, nothing is more sensitive than the question of ethnic origins in the ethnically mixed country that Turkey is, but where people nonetheless hold on to the fiction of Turkish 'purity'. Erdoğan, though, has been open about the fact that his mother's family hails from Georgia, and that the family on his father's side may be Laz, a Muslim people who are ethnically related to the Georgians and who populate the Black Sea region of Turkey. There is an ideological explanation for this relaxed attitude: for Islamists, belonging to the international community of the faithful, the *ummah*, tends to take precedence over ethnic and national identities. In that sense, they are internationalists. In a speech, Erdoğan related that his great-grandfather, a mullah, had responded to his grandfather's question about the ethnicity of the family by saying that 'God is not going to ask us to which tribe we belong. Just say, thank God we are Muslims, and let it be.' However, there are limits to this open-mindedness: what Erdoğan could not stomach was the claim, which he found preposterous, that he was of Armenian origin.

Erdoğan's 'university', the MTTB, was the ideological breeding ground for the whole generation of Islamists cadres that would later, in 2001, found the AKP. All of the party's leading figures had belonged to the right-wing student association during their high school and/or university years. They include Abdullah Gül, who was president between 2007 and 2014, and Bülent Arınç, who was deputy prime minister from 2009 to 2015 and before that speaker of the parliament. Their worldviews were forged in the traditionalist milieu of the provincial middle class, and their political values shaped by a combination of hard-line anti-leftism and aggrieved religious nationalism. Yet while a hard-line anti-leftism united the provincial middle class and the metropolitan bourgeoisie, they also had conflicting interests: the small-scale businessmen and industrialists in Anatolia were initially in conflict with the urban big bourgeoisie. The Anatolian start-ups felt they were at a systemic disadvantage because they did not enjoy the same kind of lucrative relations with the state as the established business conglomerates in the metropolitan centres or their access to credit. This was a time – the 1960s and 1970s – when

Turkey was a closed capitalist economy, in which the state played a major role. For instance, it decided import quotas. Material interests and differences in cultural outlook between the provincial and urban factions of the bourgeoisie combined to give the intra-class conflict the appearance of a 'culture war': the material frustrations of the socially and religiously conservative provincial middle class came to be 'naturally' expressed in 'Islamic' terms because the metropolitan bourgeoisie that enjoyed all the privileges was 'Westernized'. As we saw in Chapter 3, the republic that Atatürk founded was the midwife and protector of this 'national bourgeoisie'. But in time, the capitalist development that the state helped along also produced a new, distinctly religiously conservative petit-bourgeois class in the towns of Anatolia.

The dominant right-wing party in the 1960s and 1970s, the Justice Party (AP), led by Süleyman Demirel, was the political vehicle of the interests of the 'established' bourgeoisie. In 1969, Necmettin Erbakan, an old friend of Demirel since their university days, mounted a rebellion against a capitalist order that was rigged in favour of metropolitan big business. Erbakan sought and won the election to the presidency of the Turkish Association of Chambers of Commerce, which would have provided him with a platform to challenge the supremacy of the metropolitan bourgeoisie, had he been allowed to take office. However, Prime Minister Demirel personally intervened, ordering the police to physically prevent Erbakan from entering the premises of the association to which he had been elected president. Erbakan then decided to enter politics. In 1970, he would found Turkey's first 'Islamic' party. But first, he tried to work within the system and applied for membership in the conservative AP. This was how the various

Islamic civil society groups and fraternities had traditionally operated: they exerted their influence through the establishment conservative parties. But Demirel vetoed Erbakan. It is an open question whether an Islamist party would have seen the light of day at all if the interests of small and medium-sized businesses in provincial Anatolia had been accommodated, and, not unimportantly, if the political ambitions of Erbakan had not been frustrated.

Figure 7 Necmettin Erbakan, the father of political Islam in Turkey. He spoke for the provincial, disadvantaged bourgeoisie, but also for the lower, rural class.

The Islamist party occupied an ambiguous position in the class conflict that ravaged Turkey during the 1970s. While the Islamists were die-hard anti-leftists and formed a Nationalist Front with the conservatives and the fascists, at the same time they advocated income redistribution and a greater economic role for the state in order to redress the imbalance between provincial and metropolitan areas, which put them at odds with the neoliberal right. This was a reflection of the class interests the Islamists represented: their party spoke for the provincial, disadvantaged bourgeoisie but also for the lower, rural class. From the very beginning, the Islamists enjoyed strong support among the religiously conservative Kurdish peasantry. The Islamist party leader Erbakan was a mechanical engineer, with a lifelong passion for heavy industry, especially for military industry; he espoused an industrial nationalism that wedded the class interests he represented and the anti-imperialism to which he was emotionally committed. He wanted the state to invest in a military industry in Anatolia; this would both enrich the local industrialists who financed his party, and make Turkey more independent of the United States, on which it depended for its military procurements. Erbakan also pleaded for a 'just economic order' that vaguely evoked a European-style welfare state. These social ambitions and not least his anti-Americanism – along with his anti-Zionism, which was distinctly anti-Semitic – would ultimately be Erbakan's undoing; they would end up clashing with the evolving interests of the Anatolian business and industrial community, his core constituency, and open the way for Erdoğan, who wrenched control over the Islamist movement from Erbakan in the late 1990s. As we will soon see, it was the 'liberal' Erdoğan rather than the statist Erbakan who answered to the class interests of the Anatolian bourgeoisie in the era of neoliberal globalization.

Erbakan's ideal of a just economic order corresponded to a 'utopian picture of an egalitarian petit-bourgeois society'.[3] However, this vision became increasingly anomalous in Islamist ranks, not sitting at all well with the business base of the party. In 1994, the Islamist party revised its economic and social programme, and assured that the 'just order' was business-friendly. It furthermore announced that no strikes would take place once the 'just order' had been realized, as the needs of the workers would have been taken care of. By then the Islamist party, which had re-emerged under a new name, the Welfare Party, had become the leading political party in Turkey. The same year, Erdoğan was elected mayor of Istanbul, the biggest city in the country and its economic and cultural capital. The Islamists were successful because they catered simultaneously to the religiously conservative Anatolian bourgeoisie and to the working class in the metropolitan areas. They filled the vacuum that had appeared after the crushing of the left by the fascists and the military. After 1983, when the military handed over power to an elected conservative government, social democracy was legalized again, but the left never recovered. It was disabled first because the neoliberal regime restricted trade union activity, and second because it could not compete with the Islamists, who by then had laid claim to the working class by playing on religious feelings and deploying a 'social' rhetoric. The Islamists succeeded in retaining working-class support even after they abandoned the rhetoric of the 'just order' and embraced neoliberalism. They effected what one scholar has described as a 'passive revolution',[4] mobilizing the urban poor on behalf of the neoliberal project and neutralizing the challenge to capitalism. However, what still remained to be settled was the tension between the two factions of the bourgeoisie: the mainly Istanbul-based, 'secular' business interests and the 'Anatolian tigers' (to use the liberal jargon) of the provincial, 'Islamic' business interests. Those factions eventually coalesced behind Erdoğan's party. But before that happened, intra-class tensions erupted.

On 28 February 1997, the Turkish military, supported by the conservative president Demirel, addressed a memorandum to the government asking it to take measures against Islamization in the state and in society. The government, a coalition between the Islamist Welfare Party and a secular conservative party, was headed by Necmettin Erbakan. The memorandum undermined Erbakan's position, and he eventually had to resign. On the face of it, the military had intervened to 'protect secularism'. The reality was more complex. The Welfare Party's rise to governmental power had unsettled and challenged the mainly Istanbul-based capital; established big business came to fear what was called 'green capital', the new bourgeoisie of conservative Anatolia that the Islamists represented.[5] But Erbakan also, and more importantly, challenged the pro-Western orientation of Turkey, and thus threatened a vital American geopolitical interest. When he became prime minister in 1996, Erbakan ostentatiously chose to make his first foreign trip to Iran, the number-one enemy of the United States, and he continued with a visit to Libya's dictator Muammar Gaddafi, whose regime was then under international sanctions. That was what made him intolerable to the military. As we have seen, the Turkish military is not the secularist watchdog that the standard history holds it to be; it has actively promoted Islam in order to neutralize the left. However, what the generals could not accept was the Islamist-led government calling Turkey's ties to the United States into question. That was why they intervened against Erbakan. But just like earlier coups, the 'post-modern coup' of 28 February 1997 also accorded with the dominant, bourgeois class interests.

Erdoğan, then mayor of Istanbul, reacted strongly to the intervention of the military; he wanted the Islamists to resist the coup, and was incensed that Erbakan caved in and meekly resigned. Erdoğan, a fighter by temperament, had been ready to ask the party faithful to take to the streets of Istanbul, but the signal from Erbakan for an Islamist uprising never came. Once his emotions had cooled though, Erdoğan drew the politically smart conclusions from what had happened. Only six years after the country's first Islamist head of government had been forced to step down, Erdoğan avenged the post-modern coup and was elected prime minister. The key to his ascent was the realization that challenging Turkey's ties to the West and alienating the Istanbul bourgeoisie were dead ends. Erdoğan and a new generation of Islamist politicians had concluded that, to come to power, the Islamists needed to reinvent themselves. They had to embrace the West and the bourgeois order, cultivate relations with Washington, and mend fences with the big barons of Turkish business. These 'reformists' broke ranks with Erbakan, and in 2001 founded the 'conservative democrat' AKP.

The AKP achieved what the Welfare Party had failed to do: manufacture unity between the dominant classes and class factions.

> The AKP gained the support of the Istanbul-based big bour-geoisie, the small- and medium-scale bourgeoisie, especially the Muslim-conservative sections of the latter, urban Muslim-conservatives, and also some from the upwardly-mobile secular middle class. These various factions of the bourgeoisie were united by the AKP's neoliberal policies.[6]

Ultimately, it was neoliberal globalization that had brought about bourgeois unity: it had done so by changing the perspectives and interests of the Anatolian businessmen and industrialists. Their interests now converged with those of the Istanbul bourgeoisie. The locally oriented small-scale industrialists who had supported Erbakan's Islamic anti-imperialism and industrial nationalism in the 1970s had by the 1990s become major exporters to Europe, and now had a stake in the neoliberal order. Erbakan's condemnations of the 'Godless' West and its imperialism had in the 1970s given vent to the Anatolian petit-bourgeoisie's frustration at being the disadvantaged participant in the capitalist order, but such rhetoric no longer resonated with them. There was no point in pursuing a 'culture war' with the West now that they had access to Western markets. Like the 'secular' bourgeoisie of Turkey, the 'Islamic' bourgeoisie also wanted to be part of the American-led capitalist world order. Erdoğan spoke for those class interests when he declared that he wanted to make Turkey more hospitable to foreign investment and 'more cooperative with the world, at peace with it, and easier for the world to enter'. 'We are not going to take any steps whatsoever that would worry the private sector, the finance sector and that would shake their confidence', he pledged.[7] But he also played the populist card: he claimed to represent the people against the 'bureaucratic oligarchy' that he said lived in the ghettos of the rich and which was insensible to the sufferings of the popular classes.[8]

Erdoğan went out of his way to seduce the powerful business interests and show them that he had broken ranks with Islamism. In 1999, he participated in a dinner that one of Turkey's leading industrial magnates, Bülent Eczacıbaşı, hosted in his mansion overlooking the Bosporus. On Erdoğan's request, the magnate had invited the cream of the Istanbul business elite to the

Figure 8 One with the people: like all other right-wing leaders before him, Recep Tayyip Erdoğan has claimed to represent the interests of the popular classes.

dinner. The magnates must have enjoyed listening to Erdoğan as much as they enjoyed the view of the Bosporus the mansion offered. 'We are not going to get anywhere with radicalism', he told them. But Erdoğan did more than assure them that he was a moderate who would do nothing to jeopardize Turkey's ties to the West as Erbakan had done. He also pledged allegiance to neoliberalism. 'I will continue from where Turgut Özal left it',[9] he said. We met Özal in Chapter 4: he was the architect of Turkey's switch to neoliberalism in the 1980s. This was sweet music for capital. In fact, what Erdoğan offered was even better, a combination of neoliberalism and cultural and religious conservatism – Özal was a neoliberal who never really cared about Islamic identity politics, which limited his popular appeal. The business magnates recognized that religious traditions and 'spirituality' served their purpose as opiates for the working class. Among them was Sakıp Sabancı, the patriarch of Turkey's second biggest business group. We met his father, Hacı Ömer, in the third chapter, as one of the participants in the pillaging of Armenian properties on which the Turkish bourgeoisie was founded. 'Tayyip is made of dough that is essentially composed of tradition, custom and spirituality. What is wrong with that? Used with sagacity, spirituality, the traditional customs, are very important',[10] Sabancı said. American policy makers also recognized the utility of 'moderate Islam'. They had early on identified Erdoğan as a future promise. He was invited to the United States several times during his tenure as mayor of Istanbul in the 1990s. In 1996, he and his wife and children travelled to America on the invitation of Coca-Cola. A key role in cultivating Erdoğan was played by Morton Abramowitz, who had been the US ambassador to Turkey in the 1980s. There are unconfirmed reports that Abramowitz and Erdoğan met on several occasions during the early 1990s, both in Turkey and in the United States. However, their meeting in Ankara on 15 October 1996 is confirmed. The Turkish left-wing journal *Aydınlık* ran the headline 'Abramowitz prepares the replacement of Erbakan with Tayyip'.[11] The journal claimed that Abramowitz had been having secret meetings with Erdoğan since his ambassadorial tenure in Turkey in the late 1980s, and it claimed to know that he had now, as an unofficial American envoy, encouraged the mayor of Istanbul to assume a 'national dimension', that is, to seek national power. Obviously, these were only speculations, but the French scholars Nicolas Cheviron and Jean-François Pérouse, authors of the comprehensive biography of Erdoğan I have been quoting from, nonetheless observe that 'such a hypothesis certainly does make sense',[12] since Erbakan had offended the United States by making his first official visit to Iran. There is little doubt that Erdoğan rose to power with American help and encouragement. In 2002 he was honoured like few other foreign politicians ever have been, when he was invited to the White House by President George W. Bush at a time when he was still only a party leader and did not hold any elected office. But these were also special times: after the al-Qaeda terrorist attacks in September 2001, promoting 'moderate Islam' had become the United States' top priority, and Erdoğan fitted the bill perfectly.

Yet while the dynamics of global capitalism had pulled the Islamists in Turkey toward the West, the geopolitical dynamics of the post-Cold War order ironically worked in the opposite direction in the case of what had traditionally been the pillar of Turkey's attachment to the American order, the Turkish military. With the end of the Cold War, anti-communism ceased to be the glue that held Turkey and the United States together. Instead, it started to become obvious that the two allies' geopolitical objectives were no longer identical. What especially annoyed the Turks was that during the 1990s Washington encouraged Kurdish separatist ambitions in Iraq in order to undermine the Ba'ath regime of Saddam Hussein; they feared that this would eventually also threaten the dismemberment of Turkey, with the Kurds seceding from it. Indeed, many held that this was what the United States was ultimately trying to accomplish. By the turn of the millennium, top-ranking Turkish military officers were arguing that Turkey ought to revise its allegiances and seek security by edging closer to Russia and China. This faction within the military came to be known as Eurasians. They did not represent the majority view of the officers' corps, but from the perspective of the United States the Turkish military was no longer a reliable partner – it had become a problem that had to be dealt with.

The turning point was the run-up to the invasion of Iraq in 2003. The American plan was to stage a two-front invasion, from the south, from Kuwait and Saudi Arabia, and from the north, from Turkey. Turkey's acquiescence was taken for granted. American warships were approaching the Turkish Mediterranean ports to disembark the northern invasion force when, to the consternation of the Bush administration, the Turkish parliament voted against allowing the US to use Turkish territory for the invasion. Erdoğan, who had just become prime minister, failed to deliver what he had promised Bush. American officials blamed the Turkish general staff, claiming that it had not done its best to persuade reluctant lawmakers to vote yes. That was indeed correct; there was no unanimity among the generals, and quite a few had strong reservations. They feared that the Americans would not depart from south-eastern Turkey once they had been allowed in there. They foresaw that this was going to be a prelude to a Kurdish secession from Turkey under US auspices. A precedent had been set when the Kurds in Iraq were able to establish an autonomous government under an American military umbrella. We saw in the previous chapter how the Carter administration pulled the rug from under the social democrat prime minister Ecevit after he refused to let the United States use Turkish territory for staging spy missions over the Soviet Union. Neither was the Bush administration going to forgive the Turkish military for its insubordination.

In 2012, 325 military officers, among them the former commanders of the air force, navy and the gendarmerie, were sentenced to life imprisonment. They were found guilty of having schemed to overthrow Erdoğan's government in 2003. In fact, they were sentenced on trumped-up charges and on the basis of what was later revealed to have been fabricated evidence. They were all released and freed from all charges in 2014. But when the sentences were passed, liberals in Turkey and in the West were euphoric: the power of the Turkish military had finally been broken, we were told. We now have the full picture, in part thanks to transcripts that Wikileaks has made available. The US ambassador to Turkey, Robert Pearson, reported that 'Our sources within the Turkish general staff tell us that the hard core conservatives [the ambassador was referring to the Eurasian, anti-Western faction] will have to be dismissed and a modern, far-sighted [that is, pro-Western] new cadre of officers needs to be raised in order to ensure that the US-Turkey relation regains its dynamism.'[13] The fight had not been between civilians and the military, as the simplistic narrative of the international media had it; Erdoğan's government and the pro-Western faction in the military had purged the Eurasian faction that was obstructing Turkish-American relations. As planned, their places were taken by more 'modern' and 'far-sighted' officers who were reliably pro-American. This could have spelled the 'end of history' in Turkey, though not in the sense that democracy was secured; far from it: by 2012, 9,000 people – including university students, journalists, lawyers and trade union activists – were serving prison sentences for 'terrorist activities'. But for the first time since the 1950s, there were no challenges to the stability of the bourgeois order: the working class was docile, the intra-bourgeois conflict had been defused as 'secular' and 'Islamic' capitalist interests alike had coalesced around Erdoğan, and the anti-American faction of the military had been purged.

One man, however, craved more power, and his ambitions unleashed a 'civil war' within the ruling Islamic conservative elite that culminated in an attempted coup by a faction within the military on 15 July 2016. His name is Fethullah Gülen. He was Erdoğan's chief ally before turning against him. Gülen is a Muslim cleric who commands the loyalty of a worldwide community of disciples. He leads an unlikely international 'empire' of schools, media and businesses that spans the continents, from America to Africa and deep into Asia. But he also used to control a network that ran the Turkish police and the judiciary, and which reached into the military. His is a truly remarkable story and journey; it has taken him from the Anatolian backwater where he was born in 1941 to a secluded compound in rural Pennsylvania in the United States from where he has led his movement since 1999. Gülen used to address mosque congregations in rural Anatolia; he has ended up being listened to in the centres of power in Washington. How was this odyssey possible? Many pieces of the puzzle are still missing. This much is clear though: Gülen has benefited from high-level American endorsement. He can reside in the United States because powerful members of the American establishment, among them the former ambassador Morton Abramowitz, who cultivated Erdoğan, have vouched for him. Gülen is a Muslim cleric with an ideal profile from a US point of view: he is not only pro-American, but also pro-Israel and hostile to Shiite Iran. He has also built an international image for himself as a preacher of tolerance. His movement is officially devoted to 'interfaith dialogue', and he was granted an audience with Pope John Paul II. He has many admirers among American liberal intellectuals and academics.

In fact, Gülen exhibits all the typical traits of a Turkish right-winger: reverence for authoritarian state power, nationalism, an uncompromising hostility to the left, and of course embrace of capitalism. Gülen's native city, Erzurum in eastern Anatolia, is a deeply conservative place and a stronghold of Turkish nationalism, a legacy of the First World War when it was bitterly fought over by the invading Russian army and its Ottoman defenders. Gülen's first political initiative was to set up an 'association to fight communism' in his hometown when he was an adolescent. By now, the reader will be familiar with the pattern: it was their hatred of the left that led all of the future Islamist leaders of Turkey into politics in the first place. As we have seen, Erdoğan joined the fight against the left when he was only 15. As I mentioned in the previous chapter, Gülen was grateful that the military had 'saved Turkey from communism' when it staged its coup in 1980, and said that General Evren, the junta leader, had earned a place in heaven because he had made religious education mandatory. But Gülen was more innovative: his vision was to provide children from conservative families with a modern education that would give them access to the state establishment. From the late 1980s onwards, Gülen methodically set out to foster a new elite, what he called a 'golden generation'. This unabashed elitism, and the way he combined religiosity with modernity, with an emphasis on modern scientific education, conformed to the worldview and ambitions of the rising, religiously conservative middle class in Anatolia. It was a 'Calvinist' vision that validated the material aspirations of the 'puritans' of Anatolia.

When Erdoğan came to power, he relied on cadres who had been schooled by the Gülen movement. The Gülenists were already strategically entrenched in the police and in the judiciary, and they could now freely orchestrate purges in the bureaucracy and the officers' corps that opened up more career opportunities for members of their network. That suited Erdoğan more than fine. The Gülenists were fellow Islamic conservatives. But after a while they began to demonstrate independent power ambitions. Erdoğan had assumed – mistakenly as it turned out – that the Gülenists would always be his instrument; when some of his party colleagues warned him that the Gülenists were becoming too powerful, he brushed aside their concerns. He was confident, he said, that no harm would come from fellow pious Muslims. Eventually, though, it began to dawn on him that the Gülenists had their own agenda, and that they were a real threat to him. In 2012, the smouldering power struggle burst into the open when a Gülenist prosecutor – his affiliation was clear since he had been schooled by the Gülen movement – charged Erdoğan's closest confidant, the head of the National Intelligence Agency, with treason and ordered him arrested. Erdoğan, who was about to undergo surgery that day, left the hospital to stave off what was a coup attempt; 'next, they would have come after me', he said. Erdoğan announced that the Gülen movement's schools were to be shut down. The Gülenists' response came in late 2013, when the judiciary launched an investigation into government corruption and tried to arrest one of Erdoğan's sons. Erdoğan's reaction was to start a purge of the Gülenists in the police and the judiciary. He also asked the general staff to discharge officers whom the government suspected were Gülenists. The purge in the military was scheduled to take place toward the end of July 2016. On 15 July, the Gülenist faction in the military staged a coup. A military unit made an attempt to kill Erdoğan at the hotel in the resort town of Marmaris on the Aegean coast where he was vacationing together with members of his family. The coup makers bombed the parliament in

Ankara and attacked the police headquarters in the capital. The coup failed because the high command and the overwhelming majority of the armed forces remained loyal to the president, or rather, resisted the putsch that was understood to be the work of the Gülenist faction. But its failure was not a foregone conclusion; several hundred soldiers and policemen were killed in the fights between the coup makers and loyalist troops. Many details of the putsch remain unknown, but there can be little doubt about who was behind it. Gülen denied responsibility, but since the putsch occurred in the context of entrenched Gülenist influence within Turkish state institutions and a years-long power struggle between Erdoğan and Gülen, the logical conclusion is that it was the work of his movement.

All previous successful coups – in 1960, 1971, 1980 and 1997 – had, as we have seen, answered to the needs of the bourgeoisie. To recapitulate: in 1960, the obstacles to industrial capitalist development were removed; in 1971 and 1980 the left and the working class were dealt with; and in 1997, 'green capital', which was seen as a challenge to the dominant faction of the bourgeoisie, was the target. No such class dynamic was at work in 2016. No bourgeois class interests called for a coup. The putsch was an internal affair within the ruling Islamist elite, without any resonance in society. Yet it was nonetheless not unrelated to what had transpired in Turkey since the 1970s, and to the machinations of the bourgeoisie; it was the crushing of the left that had made the Islamists' rise to power possible.

I noted earlier that two conditions must be fulfilled for a coup to succeed in Turkey: first, that bourgeois class interests call for it; second, that it is openly or tacitly endorsed by the United States. The second condition was fulfilled on 15 July 2016. Conspicuously, the American administration did not condemn the putsch as it unfolded. President Obama, Erdoğan's erstwhile friend, remained silent. His secretary of state, John Kerry, briefly stated that the United States valued 'stability' in Turkey; he expressed no concern that an attempt was being made to overthrow the elected government. Erdoğan was no Ecevit, the social democrat prime minister who had the integrity and courage to reject American dictates, and who was made to pay the price for it. Erdoğan was, as we have seen, very much 'made by America', and did not challenge American interests, so there was no compelling reason for the United States to remove him. As I have shown, the Turkish Islamists have abetted American schemes. The latest example was when Turkey played a key role as the US intermediary in the war in Syria. Erdoğan's government actively fomented the Sunni Islamist rebellion against Bashar al-Assad, whom America had decided to remove from power. However, Erdoğan had become an embarrassment with his uncouth authoritarian manners; he no longer projected the image of a 'moderate Islamic' leader that had made him useful as an American tool in the first place. We do not know if any contacts were made between the coup conspirators and American military officials beforehand, but it seems likely given the historical pattern of American-Turkish military cooperation in similar situations. In any case, Obama made it clear that he did not mind if Erdoğan was overthrown.

In the wake of the failed coup, Erdoğan purged tens of thousands of civil servants. The 'civil war' between the Islamic conservatives has left the Turkish state fractured and its institutions, not least the military, weakened. Erdoğan has concentrated power in the presidency, but this is mostly a Potemkin coulisse. There are no 'Erdoğanist' cadres in the state bureaucracy or in the military that he can count on to perpetuate his power indefinitely. Erdoğan has secured his position for now by teaming up with the Eurasian-oriented, anti-American nationalists in the military, his former foes, who defeated the 2016 coup attempt of the pro-American Gülenists, his erstwhile allies; but the hard-line nationalists owe him no loyalty. He is losing ground among the middle class, as the referendum on constitutional changes held in April 2017 showed. In contrast, Erdoğan swept the working-class districts, as he always has done. Those with the lowest incomes vote either for the rightist Erdoğan, or for Selahattin Demirtaş, the left-wing Kurdish leader. Those who prefer the 'social democrat' Kemal Kılıçdaroğlu, or who say that they are 'waiting for a new Atatürk', also happen to be those on the highest incomes, so surveys have shown. But the new darling of the Turkish bourgeoisie is a right-wing nationalist, a 'grey wolf'. Her name is Meral Akşener. A sure sign of what we can expect in coming years is that the liberal Western media has started to advertise her. In 2017, the *Financial Times* claimed that Akşener is the only politician who can threaten Erdoğan. That may indeed be true. The lessons of Turkish history are clear: those who embody bourgeois interests invariably prevail. And democracy is never the winner.

Class, Identity and Democracy

'Why should it be impossible for those who call for equality and fraternity to win a majority? Why can't we come together and form a democratic bloc? Are we condemned to a fascist bloc?' The words are those of Selahattin Demirtaş, the left-wing leader of the pro-Kurdish Peoples' Democratic Party. He pronounced them in November 2016, days before he was arrested, charged with supporting 'terrorism'. Demirtaş' questions were addressed to the Republican People's Party, which represents the mainstream Turkish left. In fact, he was being polite. The question is not only why the different strains of the left in Turkey are unable to unite in a common, democratic bloc, but also why one of the candidates for partic- ipation in such a bloc has instead chosen to align itself with the right, against those whom it reasonably should have treated as fellow leftists. The social democratic Republican People's Party supported the ruling Justice and Development Party and its partner, the far-right Nationalist Action Party, against the Kurds. In May 2016 the Turkish social democrats voted to remove the immunity of members of parliament, knowing very well that the purpose was to imprison Demirtaş and other pro-Kurdish and democratic socialist lawmakers. Of course, we know why the social democratic party aligned with the right-wing bloc: as we have seen throughout this book, the Turkish progressive tradition remains beholden to the unitary nation project of Atatürk. It therefore comes naturally to mainstream Turkish leftists, the Kemalist leftists, to team up with right-wing nationalists; meanwhile, the notion of forming a 'democratic bloc' together with Kurdish leftists is simply beyond their imagination.

As long as cultural identity trumps class identity, as long as being a Turk or a Kurd matters more than common working-class interests, the left in Turkey will remain incapable of challenging the authoritarian right, and democracy will continue to elude the country. Ethnic, cultural and religious divides need to be transcended, yet that is not to say that cultural identities should be disregarded; that would be an utterly foolish suggestion. Rather, the challenge is to reconcile class and identity politics.

In fact, progressives everywhere face a similar challenge: how to conjugate identity and class politics? Chantal Mouffe, the Belgian-born leftist theoretician, observes that the 'Challenge is to ensure that the demands of the popular classes converge with the claims of feminists, anti-racists and other minorities against the elites.'[1] Turkey similarly needs a reinvented left capable of bringing together both those who suffer from class oppression and those who are oppressed because of their ethnic, religious or gender identity, because they are Kurds, Alevis or women. Mouffe has influenced Jean-Luc Mélenchon – the radical leftist who embodies the hope of the left in France – to build a movement that federates working-class and minority aspirations. These ideas also inspire Podemos in Spain.

Mouffe remarks that 'The difficulty is to create a "we" that recognizes the differences', and that 'in so far as the people is heterogeneous, there is a need for an articulating principle to federate it'.[2] However, her identification of what is, or should be, a source of 'federation' is highly controversial, and many will find it difficult to stomach. Mouffe holds that 'In most cases, the personality of the leader plays an important role. It allows for a "we" to crystallize around common affects.' She argues that 'In the majority of the political movements throughout history, the leader has always been decisive', and that 'a charismatic leader does not necessarily mean an authoritarian leader'. True as that may be, charismatic leadership nonetheless has connotations that are antithetical to a vibrantly pluralistic democracy. When the charismatic leader is held to embody 'the will of the people', intermediaries are dispensed with; popular participation in the political process is short-circuited, reducing the citizenry to a cheering crowd. On the other hand, we cannot disregard the fact that, as Mouffe points out, 'there is a very strong affective dimension in politics because collective affects play a central role in the creation of a "we"', and that this in turn 'explains the importance of the charismatic leader capable of mobilizing passions'. We have met a string of such leaders in the preceding pages. And we have also seen that, ultimately, charismatic leadership was not enough to 'change the system'.

The example of the leftist Bülent Ecevit demonstrates that the charismatic leader is indeed decisive – but only up to a certain point in the case of left-wing populism. Mouffe argues that 'ignorance of affects' is one of the major faults of the left; she claims that, 'contrary to the right, the left is very rationalist and refuses to mobilize the collective affects, the passions'. The Turkish case does not bear out this thesis. What it illustrates is that right-wing populism has been successful because it weds popular passions and bourgeois interests, while the left-wing populist challenge to the bourgeois order failed not because it was too 'rationalist', but because it elicited a violent response from the bourgeoisie. Ecevit mobilized the passions of the popular masses against the capitalist system – the only time that has ever happened in Turkish history – but his charismatic leadership could not withstand the onslaught of the system he had set out to change. Marx famously wrote that 'Men make their own history, but not of their own free will, and not under circumstances of their own choosing.' Historically, democrats in Turkey have been unable to prevail over those circumstances.

Attacking the Kurds –
The 'Return' of Kemalism

On 20 January 2018, Turkey launched a military operation in Syria's north-western Afrin district, the second time in two years that Turkish forces ventured into northern Syria to prevent what it deems an existential threat to its national security, the emergence of a self-governing Kurdish region across its southern border that is controlled by the Kurdistan Workers' Party (PKK), the militant group that has been waging an insurgency against the Turkish state for nearly four decades. Since civil war broke out in Syria 2011, the Democratic Union Party (PYD), the Syrian branch of the PKK, has carved out an autonomous region, Rojava, in northern Syria. Rojava is home to a democratic experiment unique in the Muslim Middle East: the Syrian Kurds have implemented local self-governance, set up socialist communes, introduced gender equality. This, ironically, is also the first time that a socialist-radical experiment anywhere has enjoyed American protection; indeed, it is dependent on the United States. The US equipped and trained the militia of PYD, The People's Protection Units (YPG), to fight against the Islamic State (IS), but the Kurdish militia remains Washington's principal local asset in Syria also after the defeat of the IS. Washington seeks to check the ambitions of Russia and Iran, the backers of the

Syrian regime, and has secured Rojava as a territorial foothold on Syrian soil, where American Special Operation Forces are stationed. Together with the Kurdish militia they also control the oil fields of Syria, denying the Syrian regime its main source of income.

Afrin is the westernmost part of Rojava; it is cut off from the Kurdish cantons under American protection further east by territory that is held by Islamist rebels who are supported by Turkey, and its air space is controlled by Russia. Being seen as the proxies of American power has exposed the Kurds to Russian countermeasures: Russia consented to the Turkish offensive in Afrin, opening up the air space, to demonstrate its displeasure with the Kurds' alliance with the United States. American endorsement of the Kurds upends traditional allegiances: it has brought the US into collision with its NATO ally Turkey, offering Russia the opportunity to entice Turkey away from the United States. Turkish president Recep Tayyip Erdoğan said that Turkey after Afrin will extend its operation to the rest of Rojava. That would bring Turkey into direct conflict with American troops. The two NATO allies are going to do their utmost to avoid a confrontation that would be fatal for their alliance. Turkey is not about to leave NATO. Nonetheless, since the end of the Cold War and the disappearance of the common enemy, Soviet communism, Turkish and American geo-strategic goals do not always converge; they even clash. American endorsement of Kurdish aspirations – first in Iraq to undermine the hold of Saddam Hussein and then in Syria to check Russia and Iran – has alienated the Turkish state elite; it has, as I have noted earlier, led to the emergence of a Eurasian faction within the Turkish military that argues that Turkey should move closer to Russia to safeguard its national security.

But a break with the West is extremely unlikely, in view of the interests of capital in Turkey. The natural choice for a conservative like Erdoğan is still to be the regional subcontractor of America, not the ally of Russia; hatred and fear of Russia runs deep in the Turkish right.

Turkey has pursued two goals since civil war broke out in Syria, to bring Islamists to power in Damascus and to suppress the democratic aspirations of the Kurds. In the first case, Ankara worked in tandem with Washington. President Barack Obama was grateful to his trusted friend Erdoğan, thanking 'the Turkish government for the leadership they have provided in the efforts to end the violence in Syria and start the political transition process.'[1] That was a euphemism for the services that Turkey was performing. In coordination with the CIA, Turkey provided a crucial sanctuary for the Islamist rebels and helped to arm and to train them. Officially, the Obama administration held the rebels to be 'moderates.' But the fiction became difficult to maintain when Turkey, in its effort to suppress the Kurds, mobilized jihadist militias. In November 2012, the Islamist rebels from Jabhat al-Nusra, the Syrian affiliate of al-Qaeda, launched an offensive from Turkish territory against Rojava. In October 2014, the IS laid siege to the Kurdish town Kobani. Turkey prevented Kurds from crossing the border to join the resistance. It was widely assumed that Turkey had assisted the IS in its bid to crush Rojava.

The effects of the Kurdish question in Turkey itself are poisonous as well: it helps sustain the hold of authoritarian nationalism, to which the Turkish left also rallies, disabling it as a democratic force. The Afrin operation was hailed by a vast majority across the political spectrum, eighty five percent expressing its support in surveys. Nationalism is an article of faith of the mainstream Turkish left because, as I have described in this book, it has been shaped by the legacy of the founder of the state, Mustafa Kemal Atatürk. The leader of the social democrat Republican People's Party (CHP), Kemal Kılıçdaroğlu, was quick to endorse the operation. He stated that 'our trust in our heroic army is complete, and so is our support for the operation.'[2] Meanwhile, the challenge that the democratic aspirations of the Kurds poses has pulled the Islamic conservatives into the orbit of Turkish nationalism as well. It was unprecedented, but not a coincidence, that Erdoğan, speaking on the 79th anniversary of the death of Atatürk on 10 November 2017, vowed to 'protect the legacy of Mustafa Kemal Atatürk'. It was the first time the Islamic conservative leader of Turkey referred to the secularist founder of the state by his last name, thus tacitly recognizing him as the 'father' of the nation, something he had until then made a point of avoiding. The president stressed that 'our nation's respect for Atatürk is eternal', and that 'we aim to bring the nation above the level of contemporary civilization, which he (Atatürk) pointed out as his greatest aim'.[3] I have in this book described how Atatürk laid the foundations of a capitalist state and a bourgeois order; I have emphasized that secularists and Islamists are two sides of the right, both having served capital. In that sense, there was never any break with Kemalism. However, Erdoğan's Islamic conservative party did hold out the promise of a break with the nationalism of Kemalism, which it now instead embraces.

As a young and upcoming Islamist politician in the early 1990s, Erdoğan endorsed the idea of recognizing Kurds and other ethnic minorities and granting them the right to receive education in their own languages. Erdoğan's party has a strong base among the religiously conservative Kurds. Erdoğan imagined that he could bring the conflict with the Kurdish militants to a peaceful resolution by appealing to the common, Sunni Muslim identity of most Turks and Kurds, and by granting cultural rights. It is developments in Rojava since 2012 that have been decisive in shaping Turkey's Kurdish policies, first ushering in a 'liberal' phase from 2013 to 2015 and thereafter the 'return' to Kemalism. In 2012, shortly after Rojava declared autonomy, Erdoğan dispatched his closest advisor, the head of National Intelligence, to conduct talks with Abdullah Öcalan, the PKK's imprisoned leader, on the prison island in the Sea of Marmara where he has been incarcerated since 1999. These talks bore fruit in 2013, when Öcalan called on his organization to cease fire. A 'solution process' ensued, during which the Kurdish political movement sought devolution of power to the Kurdish provinces in the southeast of Turkey, where the PKK had entrenched its control. Erdoğan was ready to accommodate cultural demands, but could not accept Kurdish self-rule, which would have amounted to political suicide for him. The military was always unhappy about the peace talks. In 2014, the chief of the general staff publicly expressed the military's displeasure with the peace process with the PKK and warned that the armed forces would 'act accordingly' if its 'red lines' – the unity of the nation – were challenged. The 'solution process' fell apart in 2015. Erdoğan adopted the Kurdish policy prescribed by the generals. Kemalism was resuscitated; the war between Turkey and PKK restarted. The Turkish army succeeded in dislodging the PKK from the cities in the southeast where it had dug in, at a heavy human cost. The elected representatives of the Kurdish political movement, mayors and members of parliament, were imprisoned. Defeated in Turkey, the PKK has chosen to relocate its forces and concentrate its political energy in Rojava. Turkey's Afrin operation is the latest chapter in the war that was restarted against PKK in 2015.

When talks were initiated with Öcalan after Rojava declared autonomy, Turkey did so with the expectation that Kurdish nationalism could be neutralized, diluted, within a 'neo-Ottoman' framework. The Turkish state persuaded Öcalan to evoke the religious and imperial unity of Turks and Kurds, who, he said, had 'been marching under the banner of Islam for a thousand years'. In a message in 2013 to his followers, Öcalan argued the case of neo-Ottoman imperialism: he said that Turks and Kurds were the 'two fundamental strategic elements of the Middle East' whose mission is to unite 'Kurds, Turkomans, Assyrians, and Arabs' in Iraq and Syria who had wrongly been separated when the Ottoman Empire was divided up by European colonial powers after the First World War. Öcalan's message was likely ghost-written by his interlocutor in the 'peace talks', the Turkish National Intelligence chief; at any rate, it was in parallel with other statements by Turkish officials at the time. A former deputy head of the National Intelligence Agency was outspoken: he said that Turkey would be in a position to redraw the regional map if it co-opted the Kurds. The Kurdish populated parts of Syria and Iraq would, so went the reasoning, join Turkey and the Kurds would be rewarded with the kind of autonomy that the Kurdish tribes had enjoyed under Ottoman rule. But neo-Ottomanism was a pipedream; the Kurdish empowerment in Rojava rendered the notion that the Kurds would be satisfied with playing a subservient, junior role in a Turkish imperial scheme unrealistic. The Turkish state elite once again opted for brute force to secure Anatolia as a 'Turkish abode'. Neo-Ottomanism gave way to Kemalism.

Atatürk is credited with having stayed clear from the military expansionism that was in vogue among his fellow dictators. A cold-headed realist who knew his country's limits, he was not a Mussolini. Yet his very last act was to prepare the annexation of the province of Alexandretta (today Hatay) in what was then the French-held mandate of Syria. The province had a majority Arab population, but Atatürk, always the professional military, was guided by what the map told – that the Anatolian heartland was vulnerable to an invasion by the eastern Mediterranean if Turkey did not have Alexandretta in its possession. Turkey annexed the province in 1939. In 2018, Turkish troops moved into adjacent Afrin from Hatay. Atatürk also coveted Mosul in northern Iraq, but the bid failed. Atatürk had misgivings about the future; he feared that Turkey's territorial integrity would be jeopardized if large Kurdish populations on the other side of its southern border were left to their own devices. The Afrin operation is an exercise in Kemalist geopolitics. It is an example of the continuity from Atatürk to Erdoğan.

Turkish Marxists have held Kemalism to be the first step to socialism; Turkish social democrats entertain the fiction that 'the universal principles of social democracy' are compatible with Kemalism. Mustafa Kemal Atatürk is a national and pro-gressive icon who cannot be casually abandoned. Yet Turkish progressives will have to emancipate from their father figure if they are going to fulfil their potential as democrats. It is not 'the soldiers of Mustafa Kemal' who are going to bring peace and democracy to Turkey.

Notes

Introduction

1. Kinross 1964/2005: 503.
2. *Birikim*, 18 September 2007.

Chapter 1

1. Karen Barkey's *Empire of Difference* (2008/2013) is a fine example of modern scholarship on the history of the Ottomans.
2. Barkey 2008/2013: 80.
3. Christian boys were levied from their families, converted to Islam and raised to serve either in the elite force of the military, the *janissaries*, or as top administrators in the empire.
4. Barkey 2008/2013: 81.
5. Kinross 1964/2005: 240.
6. Ihrig 2014: 31.
7. Kinross 1964/2005: 245.
8. Mango 1999: 291.
9. Rogan 2015/2016: 27.
10. Timur 2012/2014: 26.
11. Rogan 2015/2016: 424-5.
12. Bora 2017: 633.
13. Mango 1999: 302.
14. Mango 1999: 304.
15. Mango 1999: 304.
16. Mango 1999: 304.
17. Excerpt from 'Requiem to the Fifteen' by Nazım Hikmet.
18. Karaveli 2002: 120, 121.
19. Karaveli 2002: 122.

Chapter 2

1. Kinross 1964/2005: 348.
2. Clark 2006/2007: xi.
3. Clark 2006/2007: xii.
4. Kinross 1964/2005: 438.
5. Anderson 2008a.
6. Kinross 1964/2005: 437.
7. Kinross 1964/2005: 437.
8. Anderson 2008a.
9. Ihrig 2014: 169.
10. Bora 2017: 635.
11. Bora 2017: 634.
12. See Ihrig 2014.
13. Ihrig 2014: 115.
14. Ihrig 2014: 116.
15. Ihrig 2014: 187.
16. Ihrig 2014: 181-2.
17. Kinross 1964/2005: 450.
18. In conversation with the author in 2008, which is the source of the following quotations.
19. Avcıoğlu 2013: 214.
20. Aydemir 1971/2006: 121-2.
21. Excerpt from Nazım Hikmet's poem 'Evening Walk', written in 1950. Hikmet 1975: 60.
22. Marchand and Perrier 2013: 12.
23. *Radikal*, 24 February 2015.
24. İnsel 1990/2012: 94.
25. İnsel 1990/2012: 93.
26. Quoted in Rubel 2002: 478.
27. Rubel 2002: 479.
28. Rubel 2002: 479.
29. *Birikim*, 18 September 2007.
30. Keyder 2003/2005: 141.

Chapter 3

1. Faulkner 2013: 75.
2. I rely here on the works of the sociologist and historian Çağlar Keyder (1987, 2003/2005), which are indispensable for understanding the process that led to the emergence of the bourgeoisie in Turkey.
3. Barkey 2008/2013: 77.
4. Timur 2012/2014: 62.
5. Barkey 2008/2013: 279.
6. Barkey 2008/2013: 285.
7. Timur 2012/2014: 28.
8. Timur 2012/2014: 152.
9. Timur 2012/2014: 155.
10. Timur 2012/2014: 68-9.
11. Ecevit 1990/2009.
12. See Georgeon 2003.
13. Bora 2017: 51.
14. Bora 2017: 51.
15. Rogan 2015/2016: 164-5.
16. Rogan 2015/2016: 164.
17. Marchand and Perrier 2013: 157.
18. Bruneau 2015: 200.
19. Marchand and Perrier 2013: 161.
20. Bruneau 2015: 139.
21. Marchand and Perrier 2013: 154.
22. Anderson 2008a.
23. *Hacı* is an honorific title bestowed on Muslim men who have made the pilgrimage to Mecca.
24. Marchand and Perrier 2013: 156.
25. Quoted in Marchand and Perrier 2013: 161.
26. 'Türkiyede Burjuvazinin Serüveni', *Görüş*, December 2012.
27. Anderson 2008a.
28. This is a concept that misleadingly conjures up the image of a united, worldwide Muslim community. The notion is not only

factually wrong, it is also dangerous, serving to sustain and fan hysteria about the supposed 'threat of Islam'.

29. Michéa and Julliard 2014/2017: 35.

Chapter 4

1. Anderson 2008b.
2. Türk 2014: 30.
3. Türk 2014: 95-6.
4. Türk 2014: 79.
5. I rely here on Çağlar Keyder's classic *State and Class in Turkey: A Study in Capitalist Development* (1987) and on Sungur Savran's excellent study of the class conflicts in Turkey during the twentieth century, *Türkiye'de Sınıf Mücadeleleri* (1992/2010).
6. Karaveli 1982: 100.
7. Yaşlı 2014: 73.

Chapter 5

1. David Barchard, 'Obituary: Bulent Ecevit', *Guardian,* 7 November 2006.
2. Çolak 2016: 112.
3. For an excellent discussion on the divorce between the left and the working class, see the book *La gauche et le peuple* by two leading French left-wing intellectuals, Jean-Claude Michéa and Jacques Julliard (2014/2017).
4. Çolak 2016: 45.
5. Çolak 2016: 29.
6. The official use of last names was introduced in Turkey in 1934.
7. Çolak 2016: 29.
8. Çolak 2016: 87.
9. Çolak 2016: 70.
10. Barchard, 'Obituary: Bulent Ecevit'.
11. Bülent Ecevit, 'Aydın'ın derdi', *Ulus*, 10 October 1956. Translation by Sarah-Neel Smith. I am grateful to Nicholas Danforth for making this article available.

12. Fondation Terra nova, 'Gauche: quelle majorité électorale pour 2012?', May 2011, www.tnova.fr.
13. Anne-Sylvaine Chassany, 'France d'en haut: A Timely Warning on Hipsters', *Financial Times*, 12 December 2016.
14. Çolak 2016: 85.
15. Çolak 2016: 17-18.
16. Anderson 2008a.
17. Anderson 2008b.
18. Ecevit 1970/2009/2015: 76.

Chapter 6

1. The wolf is revered by Turkish fascists. According to the myth popular among fascists and right-wing Turkish nationalists in general, a wolf is supposed to have once saved the Turks from captivity in their ancestral home in Central Asia.
2. See http://www.diken.com.tr/demirelden-geriye-kalanlar-ba-na-sagcilar-cinayet-isliyor-dedirtemezsiniz.
3. Birand 1984: 97.
4. Birand 1984: 98.
5. *Le Nouvel Observateur*, 15-21 January 1998, 76.
6. Birand 1984: 99.
7. Aydın and Taşkın 2014: 300.
8. Birand 1984: 102.
9. Çolak 2016: 184.
10. Çolak 2016: 215.

Chapter 7

1. Cheviron and Pérouse 2016: 63.
2. Cheviron and Pérouse 2016: 29.
3. Akça, Bekmen and Özden 2014: 26.
4. See Tuğal 2009.
5. For a detailed description of this intra-class conflict, see Akça, Bekmen and Özden 2014: 26-9.
6. Akça, Bekmen and Özden 2014: 31.

7. Türk 2014: 221.
8. Cheviron and Pérouse 2016: 229.
9. Cheviron and Pérouse 2016: 185.
10. Cheviron and Pérouse 2016: 186.
11. Cheviron and Pérouse 2016: 156.
12. Cheviron and Pérouse 2016: 156.
13. Yaşlı 2014: 124.

Epilogue

1. Interview with Mouffe in *Libération*, 20 April 2017.
2. This and the following quotations are from an interview with Mouffe in *Le Figaro*, 11 April 2017.

Afterword

1. *New York Times*, 27 February 2013.
2. http://www.hurriyet.com.tr/gundem/kemal-kilicdaroglundan-afrin-operasyonu-icin-ozel-aciklama-40716791.
3. http://www.hurriyetdailynews.com/we-will-protect-ataturks-legacy-president-erdogan-122240.

Bibliography

Akça, I., Bekmen, A. and Özden, B., 2014, *Turkey Reframed: Constituting Neoliberal Hegemony*, London: Pluto Press.

Anderson, P., 2008a, 'Kemalism', *London Review of Books*, 11 September.

Anderson, P., 2008b, 'After Kemal', *London Review of Books*, 25 September.

Avcıoğlu, D., 2013, *Osmanlı'nın düzeni*, Istanbul: Kırmızı Kedi.

Aydemir, S.S., 1971/2006, *Suyu Arayan Adam*, Istanbul: Remzi Kitabevi.

Aydın, S. and Taşkın, Y., 2014, *1960'tan Günümüze Türkiye Tarihi*, Istanbul: İletişim.

Barkey, K., 2008/2013, *Empire of Difference: The Ottomans in Comparative Perspective*, New York: Cambridge University Press.

Birand, M.A., 1984, *12 Eylül: Saat:04.00*, Istanbul: Karacan.

Bora, T., 2017, *Cereyanlar: Türkiye'de Siyasi İdeolojiler*, Istanbul: İletişim.

Bruneau, M., 2015, *De l'Asie Mineure à la Turquie*, Paris: CNRS Éditions.

Cheviron, N. and Pérouse, J-F., 2016, *Erdoğan: Le Nouveau Père de la Turquie?*, Paris: Éditions François Bourin.

Clark, B., 2006/2007, *Twice a Stranger: How Mass Expulsion Forged Modern Greece and Turkey*, London: Granta Books.

Çolak, M., 2016, *Bülent Ecevit: Karaoğlan*, Istanbul: İletişim.

Ecevit, B., 1970/2009/2015, *Atatürk ve Devrimcilik*, Istanbul: Türkiye İş Bankası Kültür Yayınları.

Ecevit, B., 1990/2009, *Mithat Paşa ve Türk Ekonomisinin Tarihsel Süreci*, Istanbul: Türkiye İş Bankası Kültür Yayınları.

Faulkner, N., 2013, *A Marxist History of the World: From Neanderthals to Neoliberals*, London: Pluto Press.

Georgeon, F., 2003, *Abdülhamid II: le sultan calife*, Paris: Fayard.

Hikmet, N., 1975, *Selected Poems of Nazım Hikmet*, trans. Randy Blasing and Mutlu Konuk, New York: Persea Books.

Ihrig, S., 2014, *Atatürk in the Nazi Imagination*, Cambridge, MA: The Belknap Press of Harvard University Press.

İnsel, A., 1990/2012, *Türkiye Toplumunun Bunalımı*, Istanbul: İletişim.

Karaveli, O., 1982, *Kişiler ve Köşeler*, Istanbul: Koza Yayınları.

Karaveli, O., 2002, *Tanıdığım Nazım Hikmet*, Istanbul: Pergamon.

Keyder, Ç., 1987, *State and Class in Turkey: A Study in Capitalist Development*, London: Verso Books.

Keyder, Ç., 2003/2005, *Memâlik-i Osmaniye'den Avrupa Birliği'ne*, Istanbul: İletişim.

Kinross, P., 1964/2005, *Atatürk: The Rebirth of a Nation*, London: Phoenix.

Mango, A., 1999, *Atatürk*, London: John Murray.

Marchand, L. and Perrier, G., 2013, *La Turquie et Le Fantôme Arménien: Sur les traces du génocide*, Arles: Solin/Actes Sud.

Marx, K., 1994/2002/2007, *Les Luttes de classes en France*, Paris: Gallimard/Folio.

Michéa, J-C. and Julliard, J., 2014/2017, *La gauche et le peuple*, Paris: Flammarion.

Rogan, E., 2015/2016, *The Fall of the Ottomans: The Great War in the Middle East, 1914-1920*, London: Penguin Books.

Rubel, M., 2002. 'Karl Marx devant le Bonapartisme', Appendix to Karl Marx, *Les luttes de classes en France*, Paris: Gallimard/Folio.

Savran, S., 1992/2010, *Türkiye'de Sınıf Mücadeleleri: 1908-1980*, Istanbul: Yordam Kitap.

Timur, T., 2012/2014, *Marx-Engels ve Osmanlı toplumu*, Istanbul: Yordam Kitap.

Tuğal, C., 2009, *Passive Revolution: Absorbing the Islamic Challenge to Capitalism*, Stanford: Stanford University Press.

Türk, H.B., 2014, *Muktedir: Türk Sağ Geleneği ve Recep Tayyip Erdoğan*, Istanbul: İletişim.

Yaşlı, F., 2014, *AKP, Cemaat, Sünni-Ulus: Yeni Türkiye Üzerine Tezler*, Istanbul: Yordam Kitap.

Index

1948 UN Convention on Genocide 28

Abramowitz, Morton 199, 203
Abdülhamid II 24–5, 38–9, 79, 81–3, 84, 135
Abdülmecid 37
Afrin 213–14, 219
Afrin operation 215, 218–19
Ağca, Mehmet Ali 181
Akçam, Taner 60
Akşener, Meral 208
Al-Assad, Bashar 207
Al-Qaeda 175, 200,
Alevis 12–13, 21, 48, 60, 176–9, 210
Ali, Sabahattin 14, 33, 150
Allende, Salvador 61, 147, 174
American Special Operation Forces 214
Amiras 70
Anatolian bourgeoisie 193–4
Anatolian Calvinists 68
Anatolian civil war 111
Anatolian humanism 155–6, 157
Anatolian left 147, 160
Anatolian revolution 34
Anatolian tigers 194
Anatolian war 44, 177
Anderson, Perry 40, 43, 94, 100, 102, 105, 109, 150

Archbishop Chrysostomos 35
Arınç, Bülent 190
Aristocratic radical 129, 154
Armenian Genocide 27, 48, 50, 59–60, 88, 91, 94, 101, 137
Association of Turkish Industrialists and Businessmen (TÜSİAD) 182
Atatürk, Mustafa Kemal 1, 6, 14–16, 22–4, 27, 29–35, 37, 40–1, 43–8, 50–2, 5–6, 69, 94–6, 99, 102, 105, 110, 112, 119, 123–5, 130, 140, 152–3, 187, 191, 209–10, 216, 219
Avcıoğlu, Doğan 51–2, 54–5, 57–8
Aybar, Mehmet Ali 62–3
Aydemir, Şevket Süreyya 58–9

Ba'ath Party 52, 152, 200
Başbuğ 166
Barkey, Karen 75
Bayar, Celal 111–12
Berggren, Henrik 129
Bobos 144
Bonapartism 66, 69
Bonapartist state 69
Bourgeois revolution 6, 68
Brandt, Willy 170, 172
British Labour Party 147, 154
Brzezinski, Zbigniew 174–76

Bureaucratic oligarchy 197
Bush, George W. 57, 200–1

Carter, Jimmy 172, 185
Carter administration 201
Caudillo 127, 150
Cemal, Hasan 10
Cheney, Dick 56
Cheviron, Nicolas 188, 199
Christopher, Warren 172–4
CIA 172, 175, 215
Cilicia 44, 92–3, 96
Circassians 24, 85
Clark, Bruce 36
Clinton, Bill 143
Clinton, Hillary 143
Çoban Sülü 109
Cold War 6, 50, 110, 124, 149,
    171–2, 174–5, 200, 214
Committee of Union and
    Progress/Young Turks 24–5,
    27–8, 48, 83–6, 88, 181
Communist International 45
Communist Party of Turkey
    (TKP) 11, 16, 24, 28, 30,
    44–6, 50, 58, 113
Compradors 73, 77, 84, 103
Crete 55
Cuban Missile crisis 171
Çukurova 92–3, 96–8

Dashnak, Armenian nationalist
    party 25
Deep State 10, 31, 49
Demirel, Süleyman 15, 53, 106,
    108–9, 147, 163–5, 183,
    191–2, 195

Demirtaş, Selahattin 160–1,
    208–9
Democrat Party (DP) 53,
    104–11, 113–14
Democratic Party 148
Democratic Union Party (PYD)
    213
Dersim 48
Devshirme 19
Dink, Hrant 48–9
Donne, John 139
Dönme/Dönmes 180–1

Ecevit, Bülent 43, 65, 81–2, 104,
    109, 129–42, 144–59, 161–6,
    168–70, 172–6, 178–80,
    182–5, 201, 211–12
Ecevit, Fahri 146
Eczacıbaşı, Bülent 197
Edward VIII 50
Eisenhower, Dwight D. 120
El Turco 18
Eliot, T.S. 140
Engels, Friedrich 27, 66, 69, 71,
    81
English socialism 139
Employee socialism 154
Erbakan, Necmettin 15, 191–3,
    195–7
Erdoğan, Recep Tayyip 1–4, 6,
    10, 15, 21, 56–7, 64–5, 67–8,
    90, 94, 96–7, 102, 108–9,
    115–17, 121, 127, 131, 134,
    160–1, 186, 188–90, 193–7,
    199–208, 214–15, 216–17,
    219

Eurasian faction, 200, 202, 208
European Central Bank 122
European Enlightenment 41
European Monetary Union 122
Evren, Kenan 134, 176, 185–7, 204

Faulkner, Neil 70
First Balkan War 26, 95
Franco, Francisco 43, 150
Frank, Thomas 4
French Annales school 54
French Socialist Party 144
French Revolution 40, 102
Friedman, Milton 183

Gaddafi, Muammar 195
Gagauz Turks 41
George, David Lloyd 17
Gezi protests 13, 115
Ghazi 22
Golden generation 204
Gökçen, Sabiha 48
Green capital 195
Grey Wolves 119, 163–4, 166–7, 176–9, 185
Guesde, Jules 104
Guilluy, Christophe 144
Gül, Abdullah 190
Gülen, Fethullah 186, 203–6, 208
Gülenists 54, 186, 204–6, 208
Günaltay, Şemsettin 119
Güneş, Hasan Fehmi 12

Hacı Emin Pasha 135

Haig, Alexander 180
Helikon 138
Hellenistic 17, 19
Hikmet, Nazım 32–4, 59
Historical mistake 104, 133
Hitler, Adolf 46–7
Hussein, Saddam 200, 214
Hüsnü, Şefik 45–6

Ihrig, Stefan 47
Illiberal democracy 2
IMF 183
Industrial democracy 153, 169
Industrial nationalism 193
İnsel, Ahmet 65, 99
İnönü, İsmet 14, 46, 48, 102, 112, 114, 130, 140, 149, 150–1
İpekçi, Abdi 180–1
Islamic State 10, 213, 215
Istanbul bourgeoisie 196–7

Jabhat al-Nusra 215
Janisarries 21
Jihad 39
John Paul II 181, 203
Just economic order 193–4
Justice and Development Party (AKP) 65, 68, 109, 161, 188, 190, 196, 209
Justice Party (AP) 53, 125, 128, 163, 191

Kahraman, İsmail 188
Karabekir, Kazım 30
Karaoğlan 162

Kasapyans 96
Kemal, Yaşar 93, 98–9
Kemalism 5–7, 13, 15, 40–1,
    43–7, 49–55, 57–8, 60–3, 65,
    100–2, 104, 107, 111, 119,
    124, 152, 181, 210, 216–17,
    219
Kemalist geopolitics 219
Kennedy, John F 171
Kennedy, Robert F 129
Kerry, John 207
Keynesianism 61
Kılıçdaroğlu, Kemal 208, 216
Kısakürek, Necip Fazıl 64
Kinross, Patrick 3, 41
Kissinger, Henry 174
Kreisky, Bruno 172
Khruschev, Nikita 171
Kurdistan Workers' Party
    (PKK) 131, 159–60, 213,
    217–18
Kurdish Kennedy 161
Küçükömer, İdris 63

Labour Party of Turkey (TİP)
    52, 54, 62–3, 148, 150, 165
Laz 189
Lenin, Vladimir 22–3
Lewis, Bernard 40
Liberal populism 105, 109, 113
Lumpenproletariat 67
Lycée de Galatasaray 24

Magna Carta 72
Mango, Andrew 30–1
Marchand, Laure 98

Marx, Karl 27, 42–3, 66–7, 69,
    71, 77–9, 81, 91, 212
Marxism 62, 154
Marxism-Leninism 124
Mahmud II 40
Mehmed VI 21
Mehmet II 71
Meiji restoration 72
Melikats 92
Mélenchon, Jean-Luc 210
Menderes, Adnan 53, 108,
    111–17, 119–21
Menem, Carlos 18
Miliband, Ralph 69
Milli Şef 150
Mithat Pasha 79–82, 153
Motherland Party 126
Mouffe, Chantal 210–11
Mujahedin 175
Muslim Brotherhood 38
Mussolini, Benito 46–7, 219
Mustafa Şükrü Efendi 135–6

Nakshibendi fraternity 126–7
Napoleon III (Louis Bonaparte)
    66–7
National Intelligence Agency
    (MİT) 205, 217–18
Nationalist Action Party
    (MHP) 163, 166, 178, 209
Nationalist-bourgeois 1–2
National Salvation Party (MSP)
    126, 163
National Turkish Student
    Association (MTTB)
    188–90

Nationalist Front government 163–6, 168, 192
NATO 50, 54–5, 121, 149, 170–1, 180, 214
Nazım, Mehmed 86
Nejat, Ethem 24, 30
Neo-liberalism 7, 61, 132, 194, 198
Neoliberal dictatorship 2
Neoliberal economics 126
Neoliberal model 184
Neoliberal policies 183, 196
Neoliberal project 194
Neoliberal regime 194
Neoliberal revolution 126
Neoliberal right 193
Neoliberal globalization 68, 152, 193, 196
Neo-Ottomanism 218–19
Nixon administration 174
Nordpolitik 170
Nurettin Pasha 35

Obama, Barack 13, 207, 215
Obama administration 215
Ottoman Naval School 32
Öcalan, Abdullah 131, 217–18
Osman 17–19
Osmanlı, 20
Ostpolitik 170
Öz, Doğan 164
Özal, Turgut 15, 126–7, 198

Palme, Olof 129, 154, 172
Pan-Turkic fascism 189
Pan-Turkic Empire 166

Paris Commune 42, 104
Passive revolution 194
Pearson, Robert 202
Peker, Recep 46
Peoples' Democratic Party (HDP) 9, 160–1, 209
People's Protection Units (YPG) 213
Perrier, Guillaume 98
Pérouse, Jean-François 188, 199
Pinochet, Augusto 61
Podemos 210
Post-modern coup 195
Poulantzas, Nicos 69
Pound, Ezra 140

Reagan, Ronald 61, 126, 180
Republican People's Party (CHP) 6, 14, 46, 52, 105, 111–15, 119, 123–5, 130, 133–4, 139–40, 144, 146, 148–52, 154–5, 164, 169, 209, 216
Revolutionary Trade Union Confederation (DİSK) 165, 179, 183–5
Robert College 134
Rogan, Eugene 27
Rojava 213–14, 215, 217–18
Roosevelt, Franklin Delano 50
Russian Revolution 16

Sabancı, Hacı Ömer 96–9, 198
Sabancı, Sakıp 97, 198–9
Sait, Sheikh 38, 45
Sadat, Anwar 187

Şakir, Bahaeddin 86
SALT 2, 172–3
Sanders, Bernie 148
Sazonov, Sergei 86
Scandinavian socialism 154
School of Oriental and African
    Studies 140
Selçuk, Ilhan 55–7, 136
Selim I 21
Servan-Schreiber, Jean-Jacques
    129
Social Democratic Party of
    Sweden 154
Socialist International 6
Soldiers of Mustafa Kemal 6,
    219
Soviet Communist Party 45
Soviet communism 214
Stalin, Josef 14
Su, Ruhi 11
Sultan-Galiev, Mirsaid 29
Summers, Lawrence 143
Suphi, Mustafa 16, 24, 28–31
Swedish model 154
Swedish Trade Union
    Organization (LO) 153
Sweet democracy 56, 63

Tagore, Rabindranath 140
Talat Pasha 49, 86, 88–90, 93–4
Talibans 175
Tanrıöver, Hamdullah Suphi
    123–4

Terra Nova 144
Thatcher, Margaret 61, 126
Treaty of Lausanne 36
Treaty of Moscow 23
Trudeau, Pierre 129
Truman, Harry S. 124
Trump, Donald 142–3
Turkish abode 219
Turkish Association of
    Chambers of Commerce
    191
Turkish Enlightenment 55–6
Turkish Führer 46
Turkish-Islamic synthesis 127,
    186
Turkish social democracy 133
Turkish State Directorate of
    Religious Affairs 135
Türkeş, Alparslan 118, 121, 166,
    178
Türkler, Kemal 184

Ummah 40, 190
United Nations 160
US Sixth Fleet 188

Vance, Cyrus 173
Völkisch 47, 49

Wall Street 148
Warsaw Pact 170
Welfare Party 194–5
World Bank 183